Bridge to Paradise

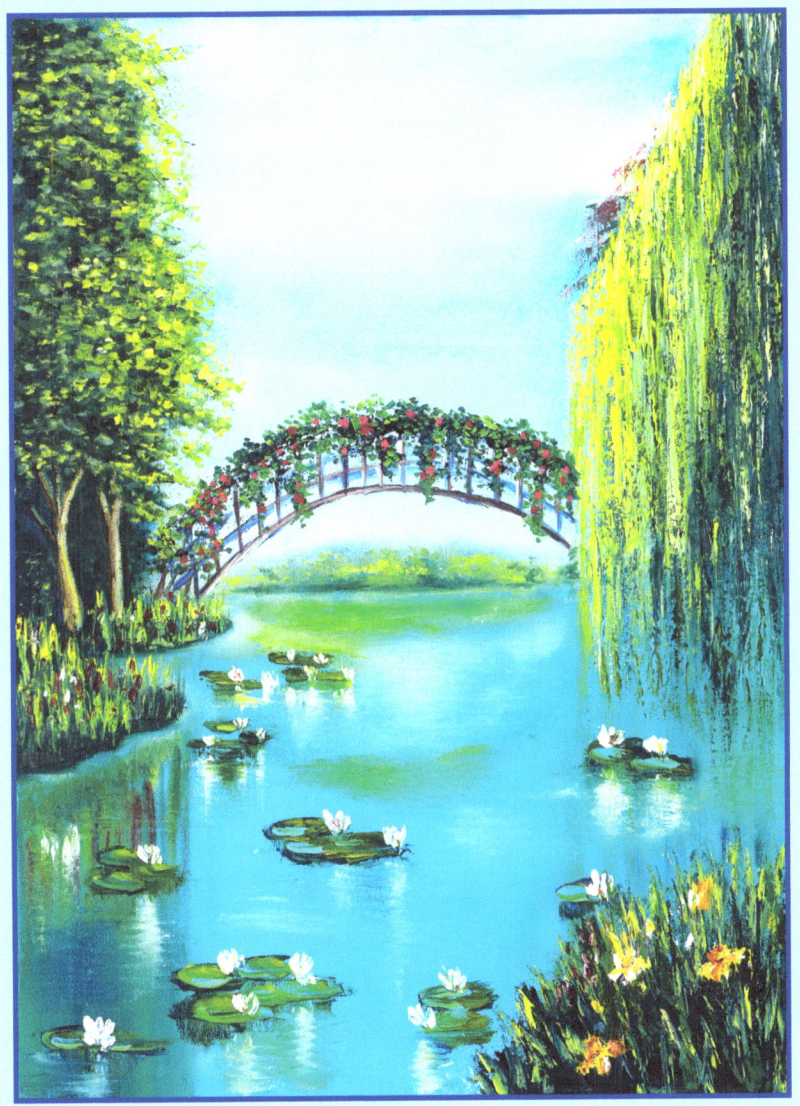

~ Art and Poetry ~

by Andrew Nazareth and Michelle Nazareth

Bridge to Paradise

Copyright © 2018 Art and Poetry by Michelle and Andrew Nazareth

All rights reserved. No part of this book may be reproduced, stored in a retrieval system, or transmitted, in any form or by any means, electronic, mechanical, photocopying, recording, or otherwise, without the written prior permission of the authors, except in the case of low resolution reproductions embodied in critical articles and reviews.

Book design by River Sanctuary Graphic Arts

Printed in the United States of America

ISBN 978-1-935914-83-9 (Softcover)

ISBN 978-1-935914-84-6 (Hardcover)

Additional copies available from:

www.riversanctuarypublishing.com

Amazon.com

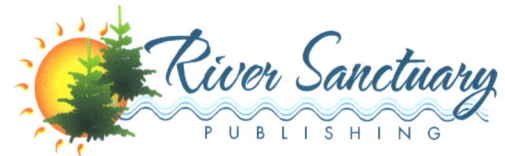

RIVER SANCTUARY PUBLISHING
P.O. Box 1561
Felton, CA 95018
www.riversanctuarypublishing.com
Dedicated to the awakening of the New Earth

To

Dad and Mom

Acknowledgments

Many thanks to David Weiss and Annie Elizabeth Porter for their amazing vision to bring this book to reality as editors. We are grateful to Shirley Lehner-Rhoades and Svetlana Semenova, for inspiring us to be artists, teaching us artistic technique and developing our artistic skills, while giving us the freedom to express ourselves creatively.

Our thanks to Mahesh Junnarkar and David Reese for capturing the essence of our paintings in their brilliant photography.

Finally, we are very appreciative of the constant encouragement and loving support that we've received during our journey, from our parents Kevin and Melanie Nazareth.

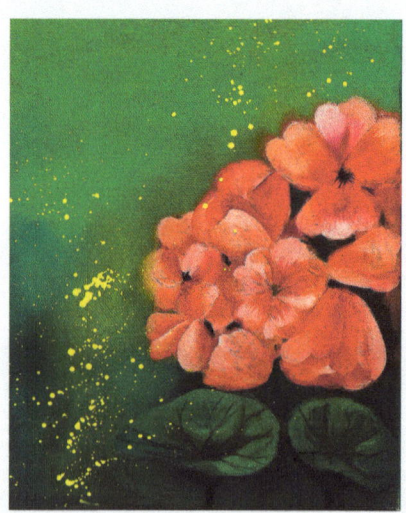

Catalog

Wavelets Under a Blazing Sun – Andrew   2-3

Ducks in the Wind – Michelle   4-5

Autumn Cityscape – Andrew   6-7

Human Light – Michelle   8-9

Birches in the Woods – Andrew   10-11

Venezia! – Michelle   12-13

JFK – Andrew   14-15

Starry Night – Michelle   16-17

Geometrical Vases – Andrew   18-19

Rocks in the Sea – Michelle   20-21

Sails – Michelle   22-23

Trees by a Stream – Andrew   24-25

imagination – Michelle   26-27

Fury – Andrew   28-29

Flowers in a Vase – Michelle   30-31

Italian Village – Andrew   32-33

Strung on a String – Michelle   34-35

Cherry Blossoms – Andrew   36-37

Bridge to Paradise – Michelle   38-39

Flight of the Hummingbird – Michelle   40-41

Northern Lights – Andrew and Michelle   42-43

About the Artists   44

Wavelets Under a Blazing Sun

The sun sets with a fiery blaze
While wavelets ebb and flow
Like youth mesmerized under a haze
Not knowing which way to go

Andrew Nazareth
Oil on canvas

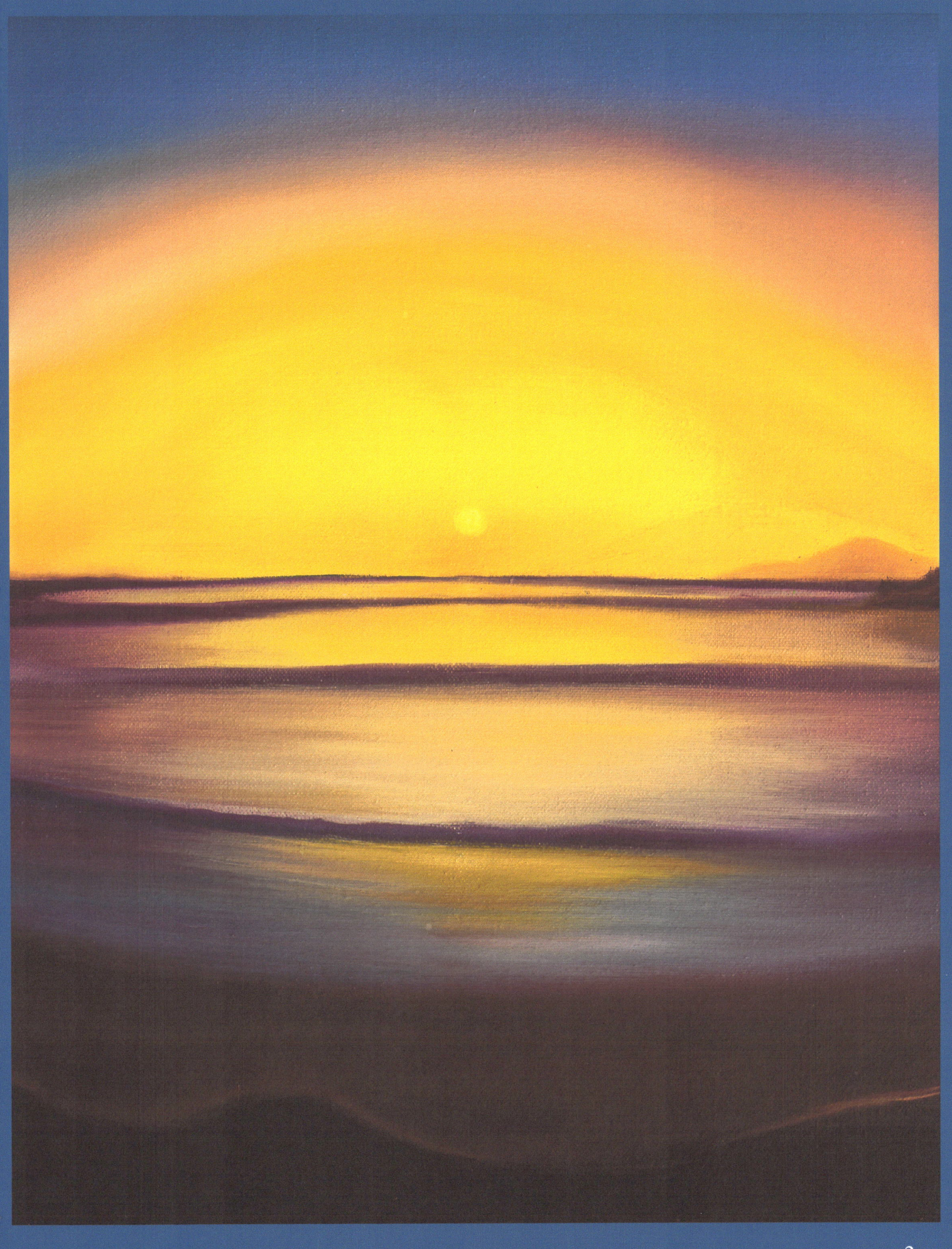

Ducks in the Wind

An old duck waddles
Sunlight shines bright on his back
He is young again

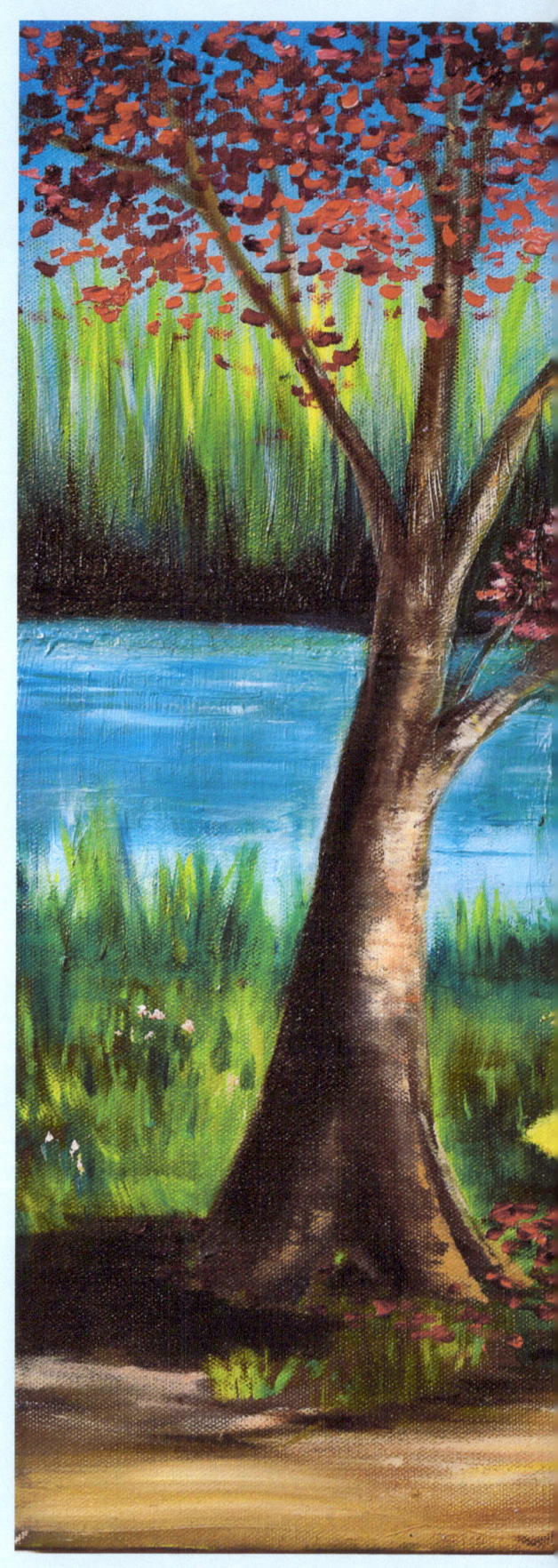

Michelle Nazareth
Oil on canvas

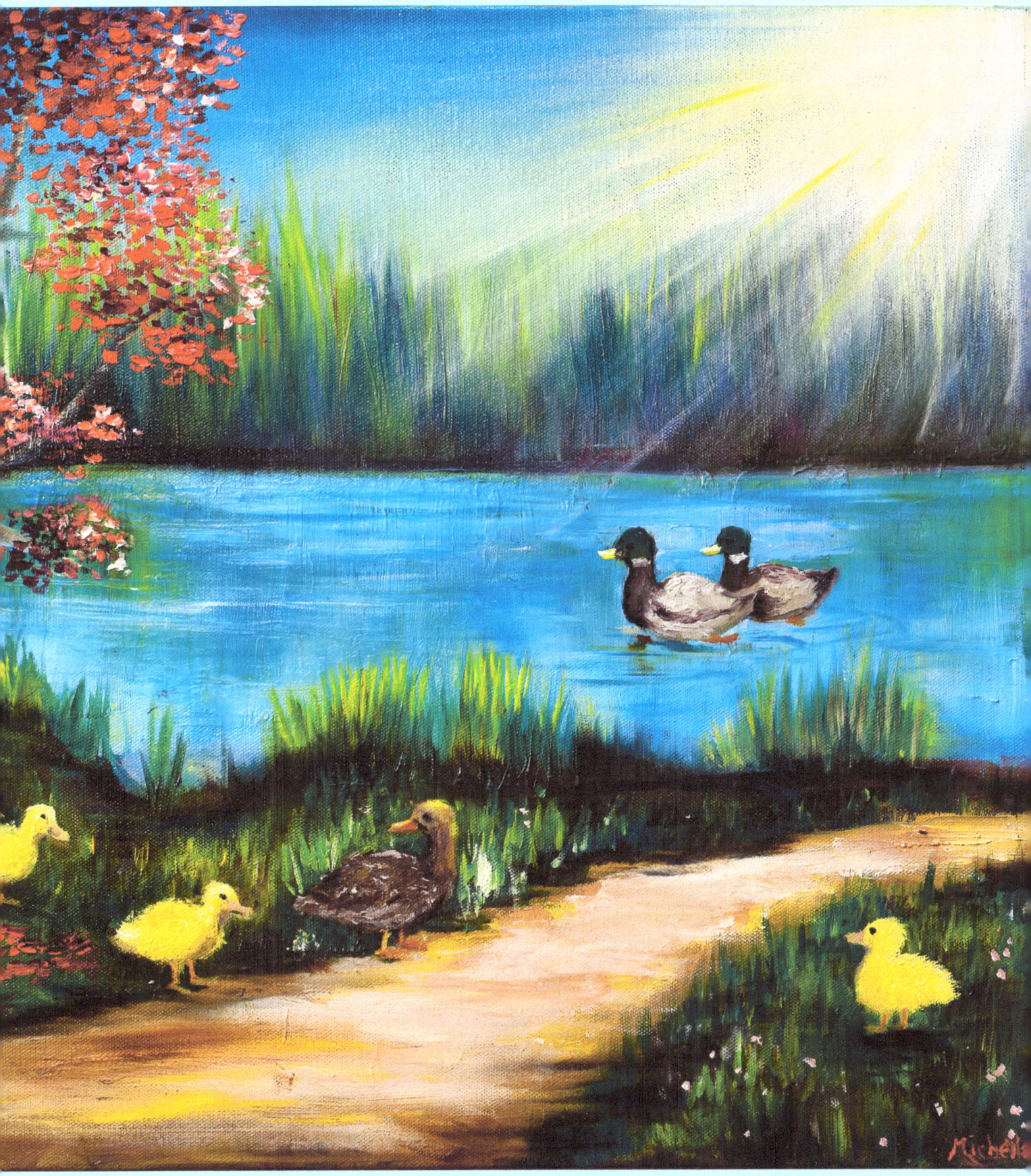

Autumn Citiscape

The glow of autumn
Shimmers on city buildings
Sprinkling golden hue

Andrew Nazareth
Oil on canvas

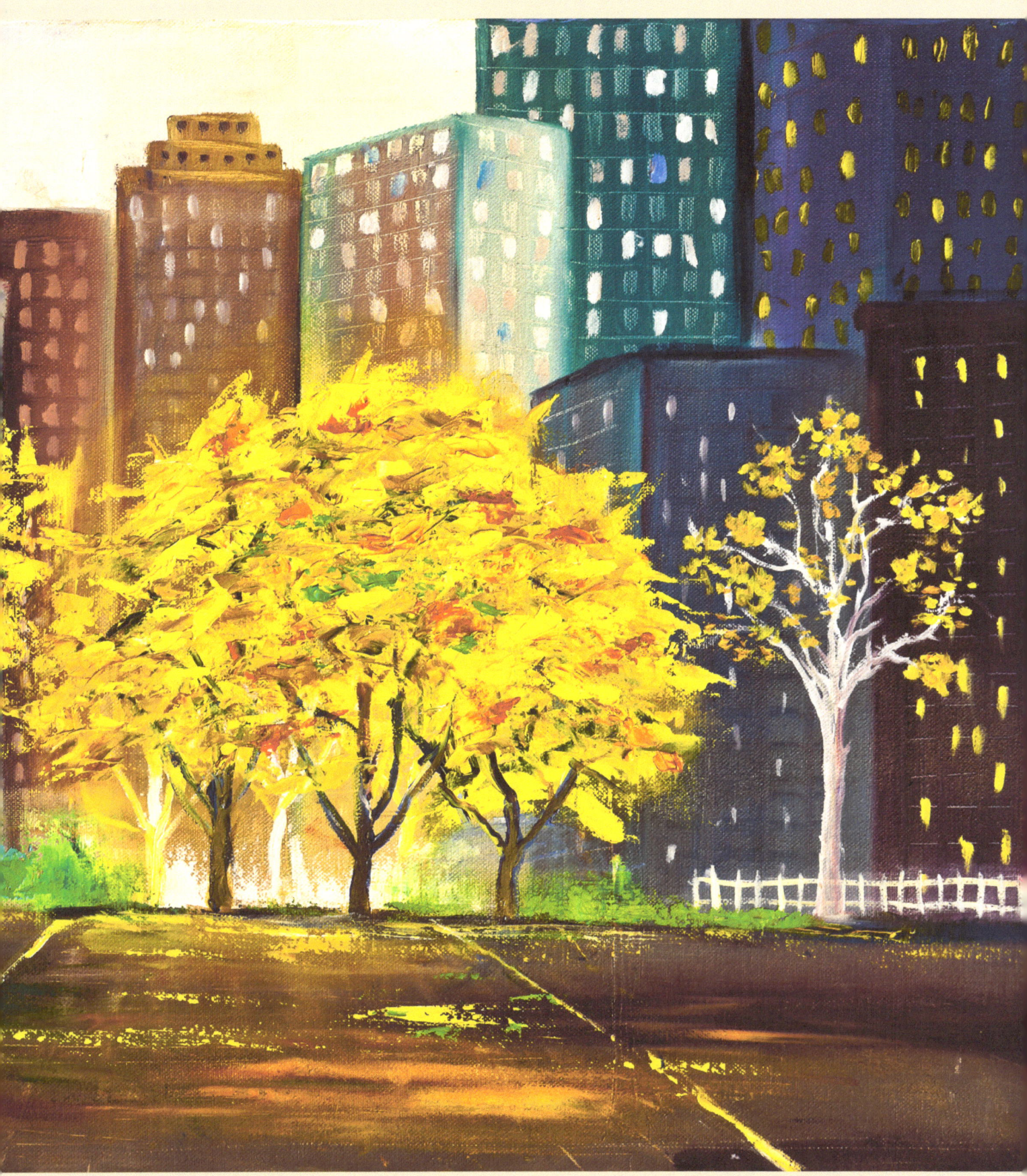

Human Light

We light up the world
Inch. By. Inch.
Strike flint & steel
Sparks!
Until we all glow brightly
From within

Michelle Nazareth
Oil on canvas

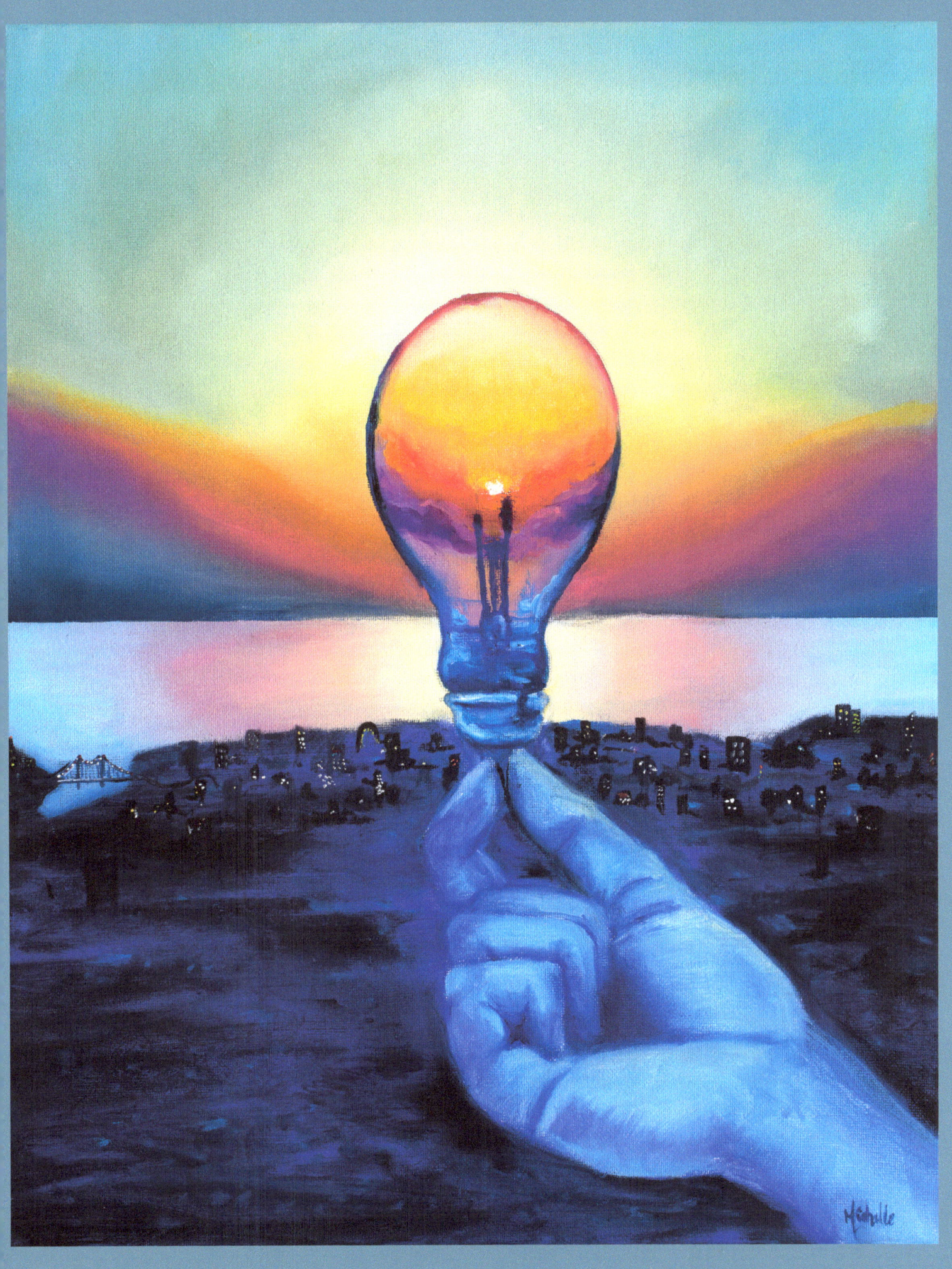

Birches in the Woods

Birches inspire young and old
Enjoying the gentle breeze
Standing tall with firm roots

Andrew Nazareth
Oil on canvas

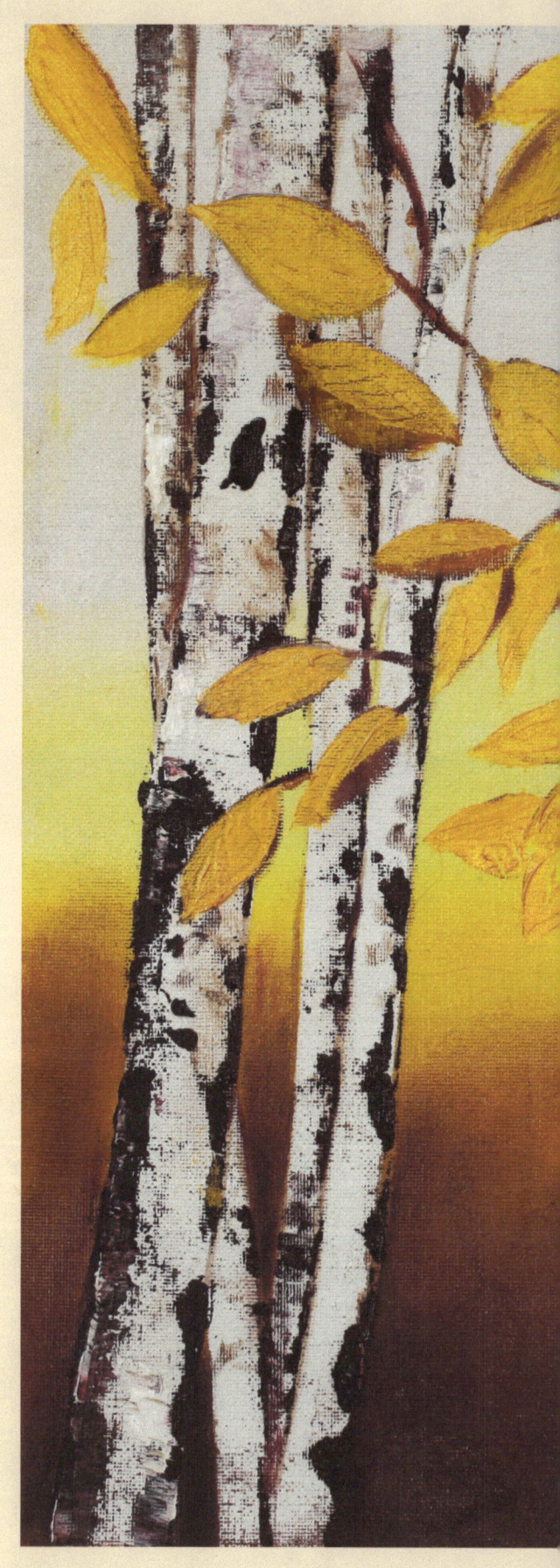

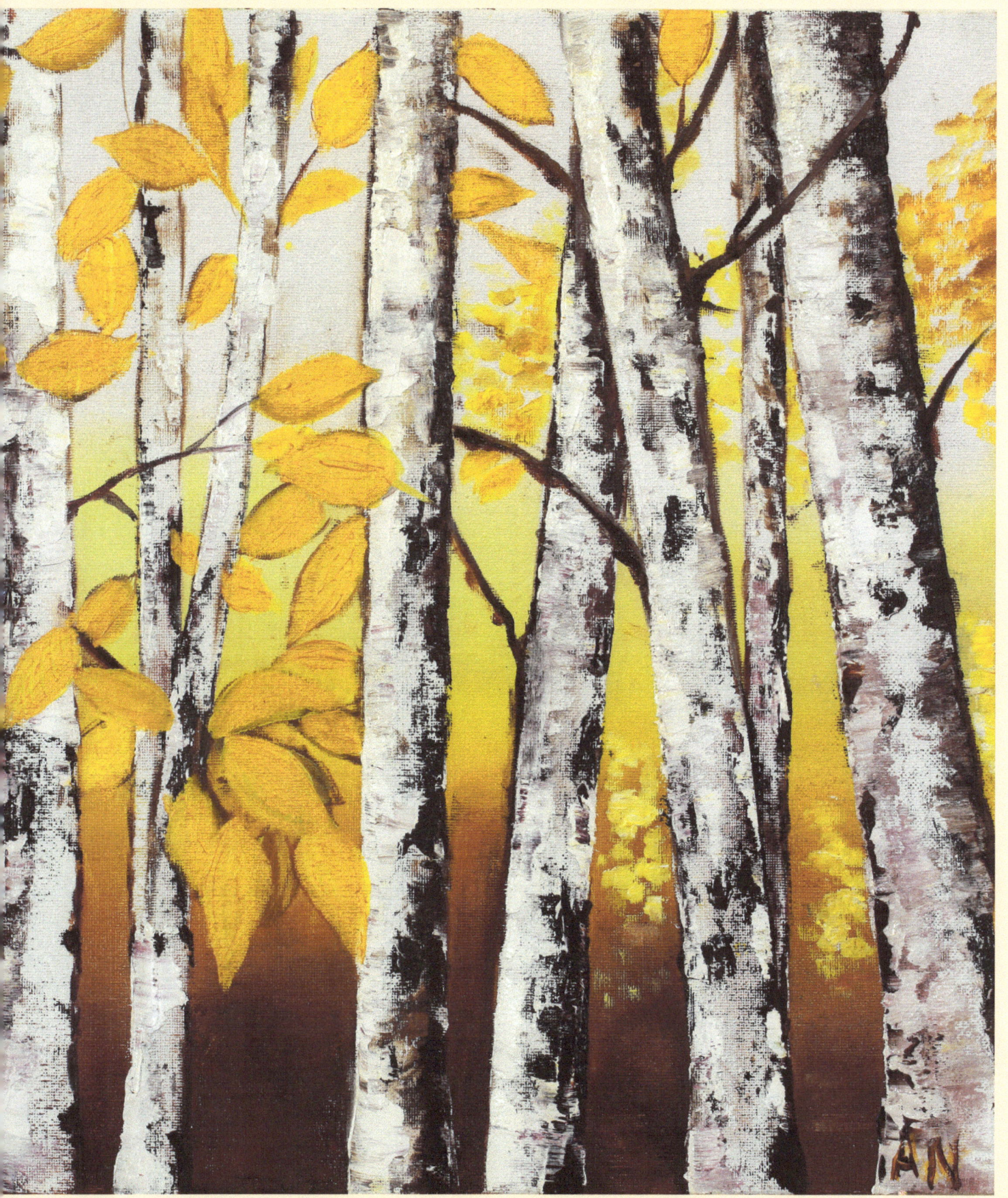

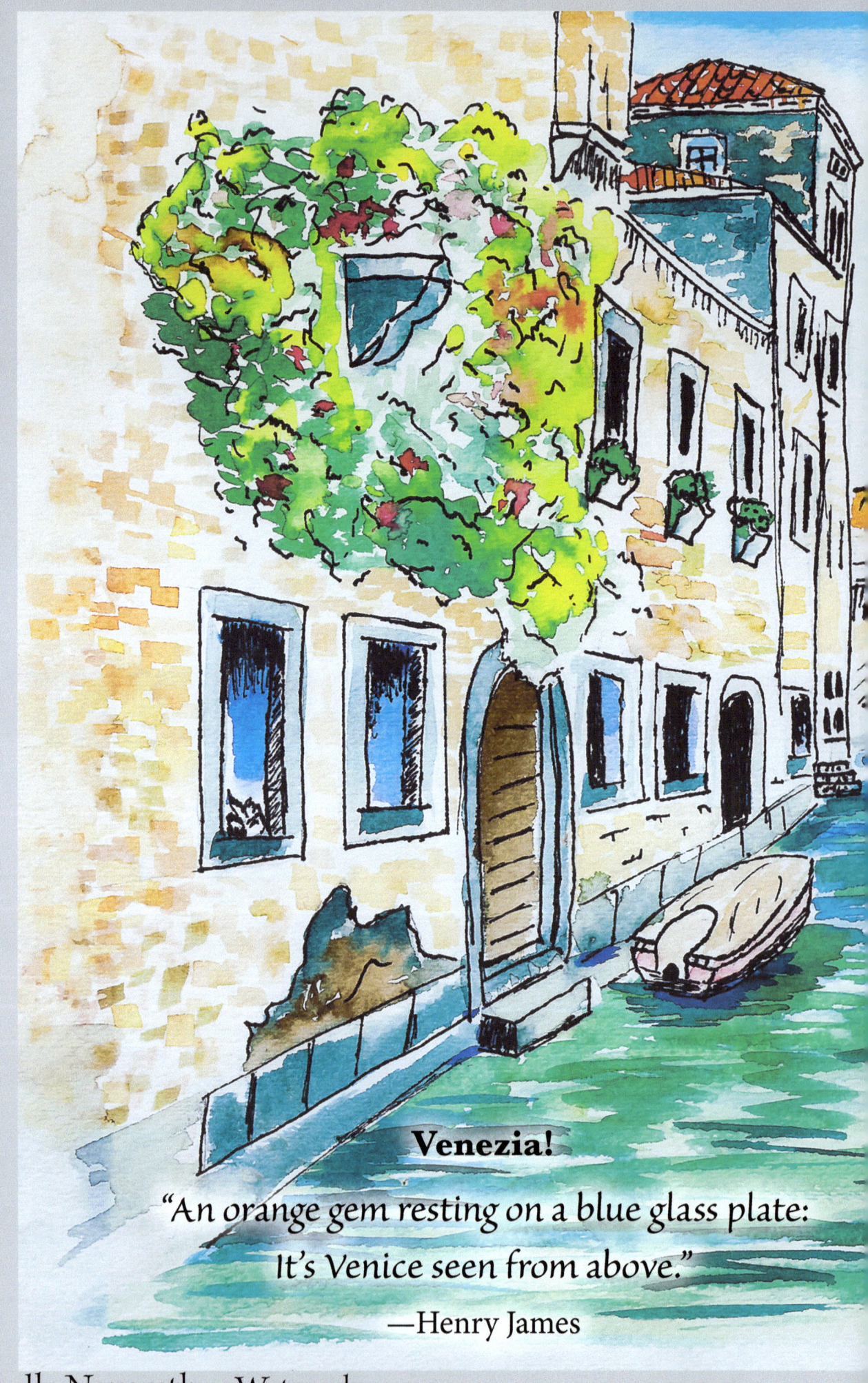

Venezia!

"An orange gem resting on a blue glass plate:
It's Venice seen from above."
—Henry James

Michelle Nazareth   Watercolor

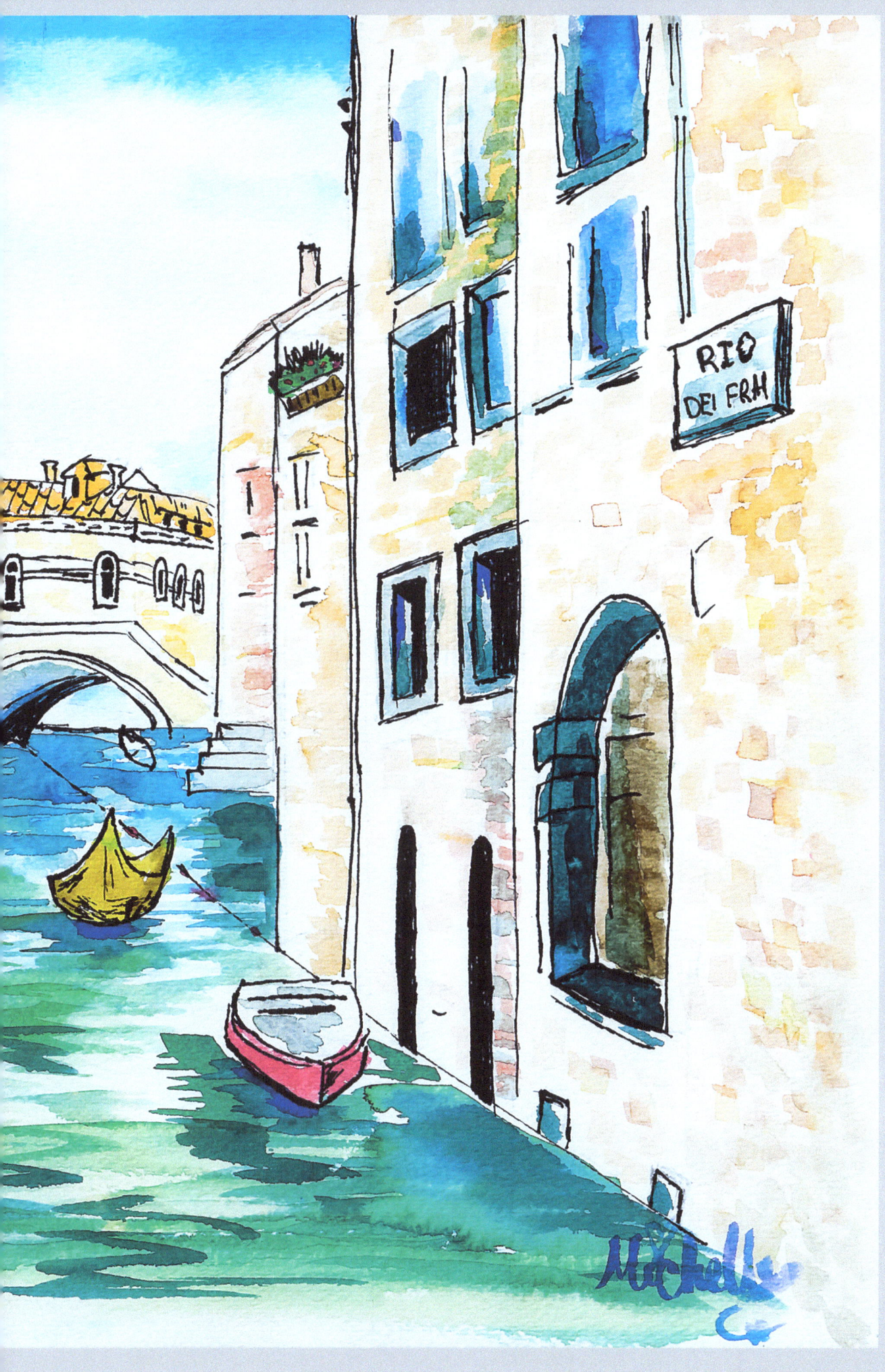

JFK

"Those who dare to fail miserably
can achieve greatly."
—John F. Kennedy

Andrew Nazareth
Pencil

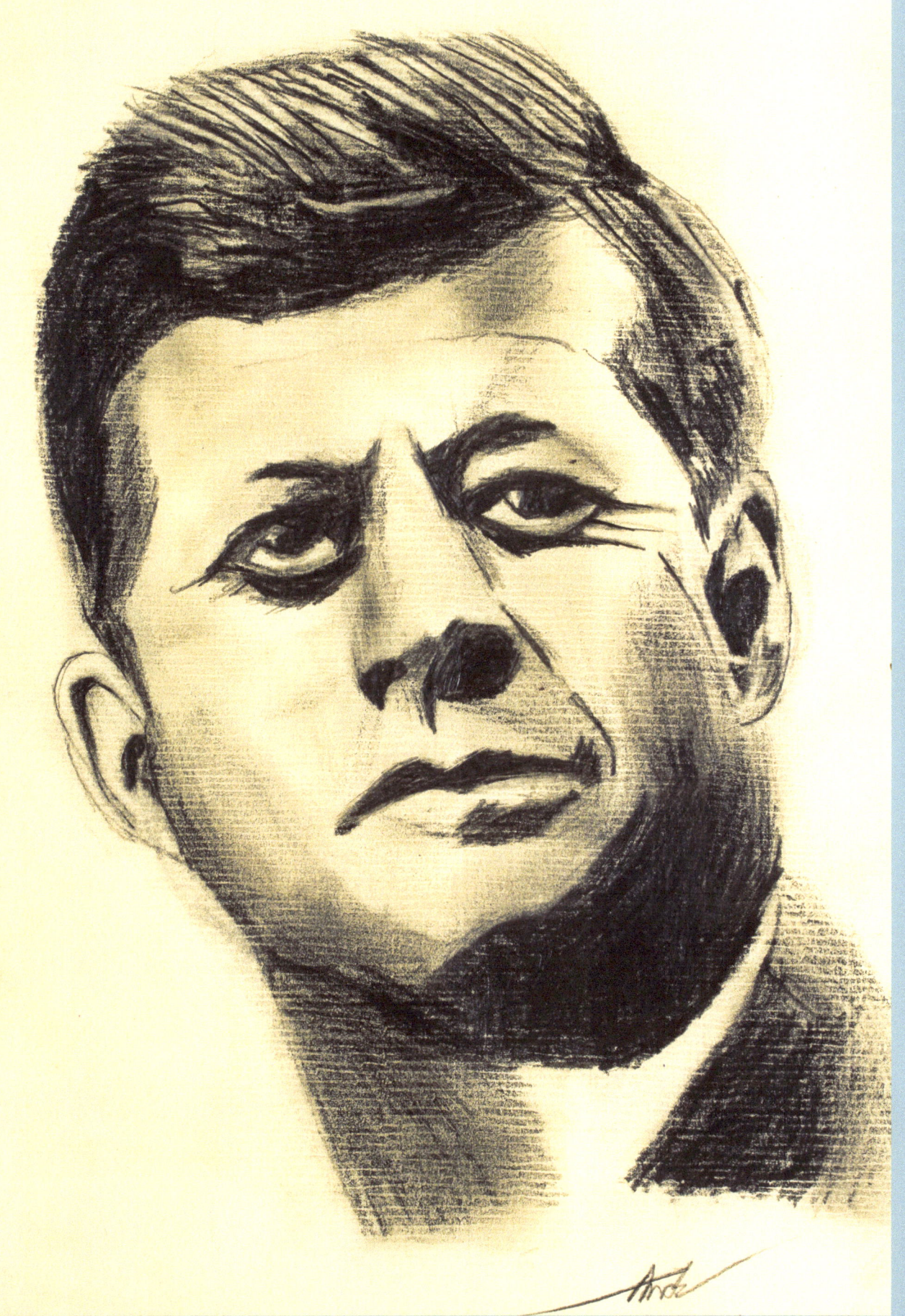

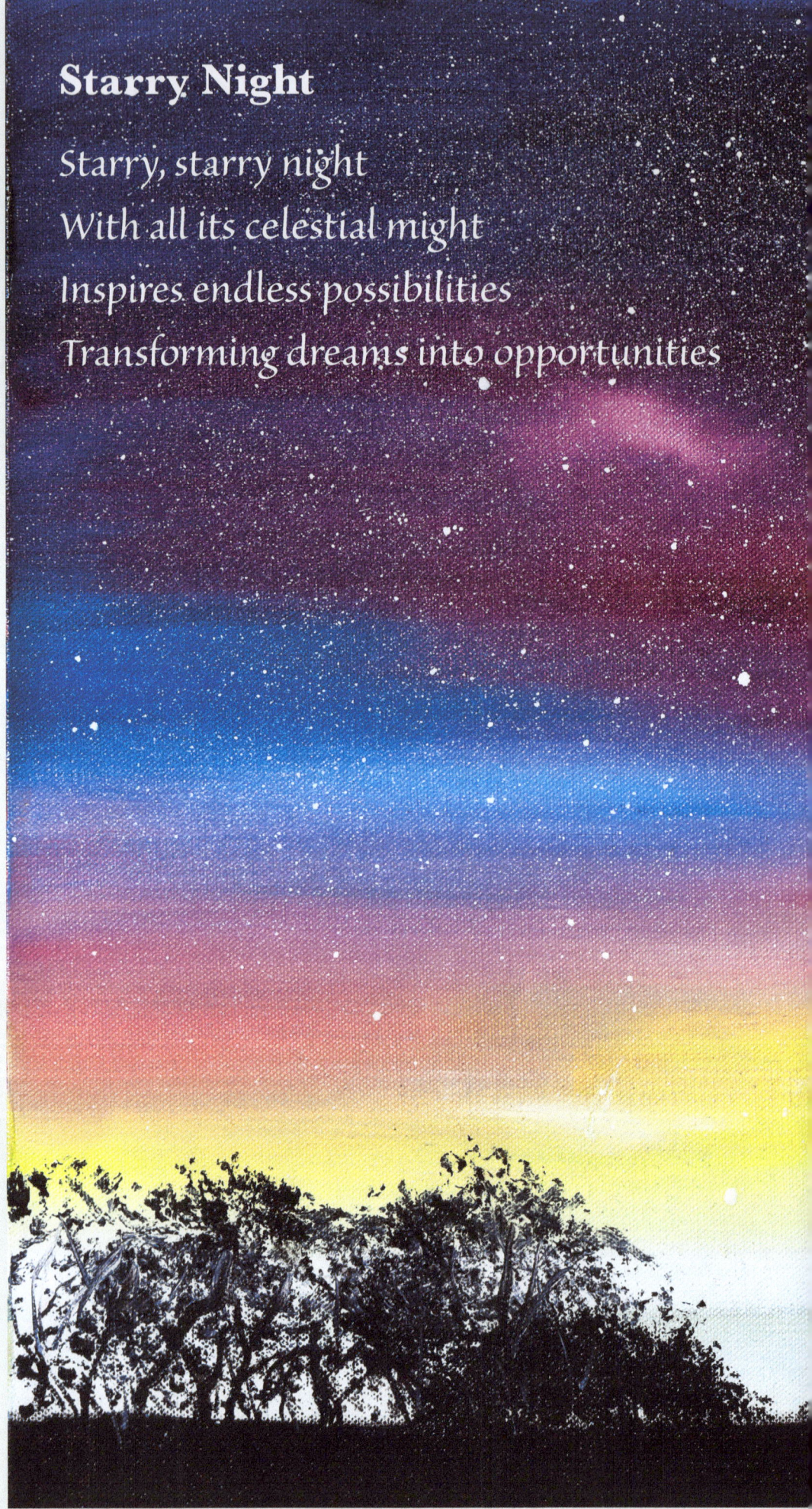

Starry Night

Starry, starry night
With all its celestial might
Inspires endless possibilities
Transforming dreams into opportunities

Michelle Nazareth
Oil on canvas

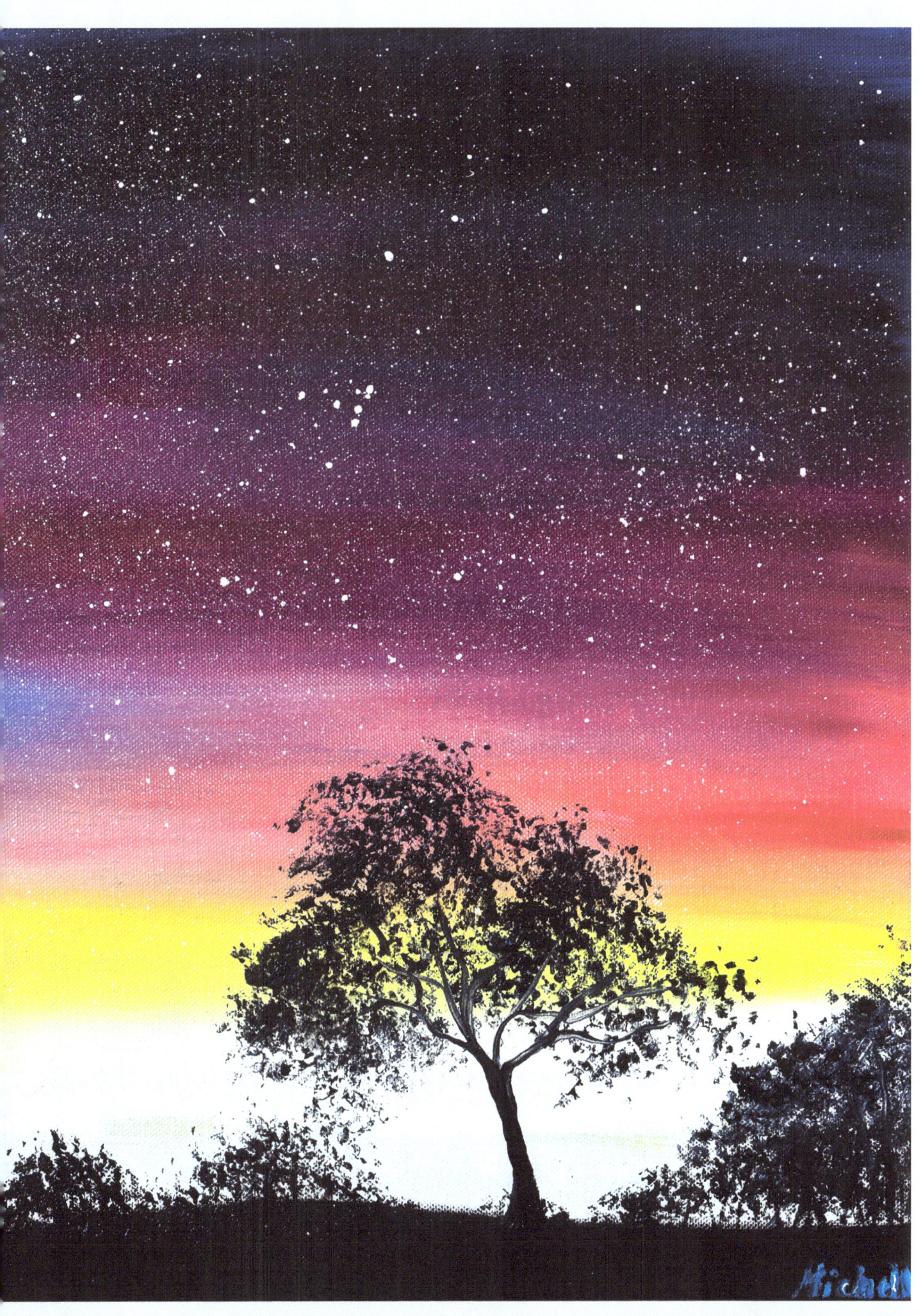

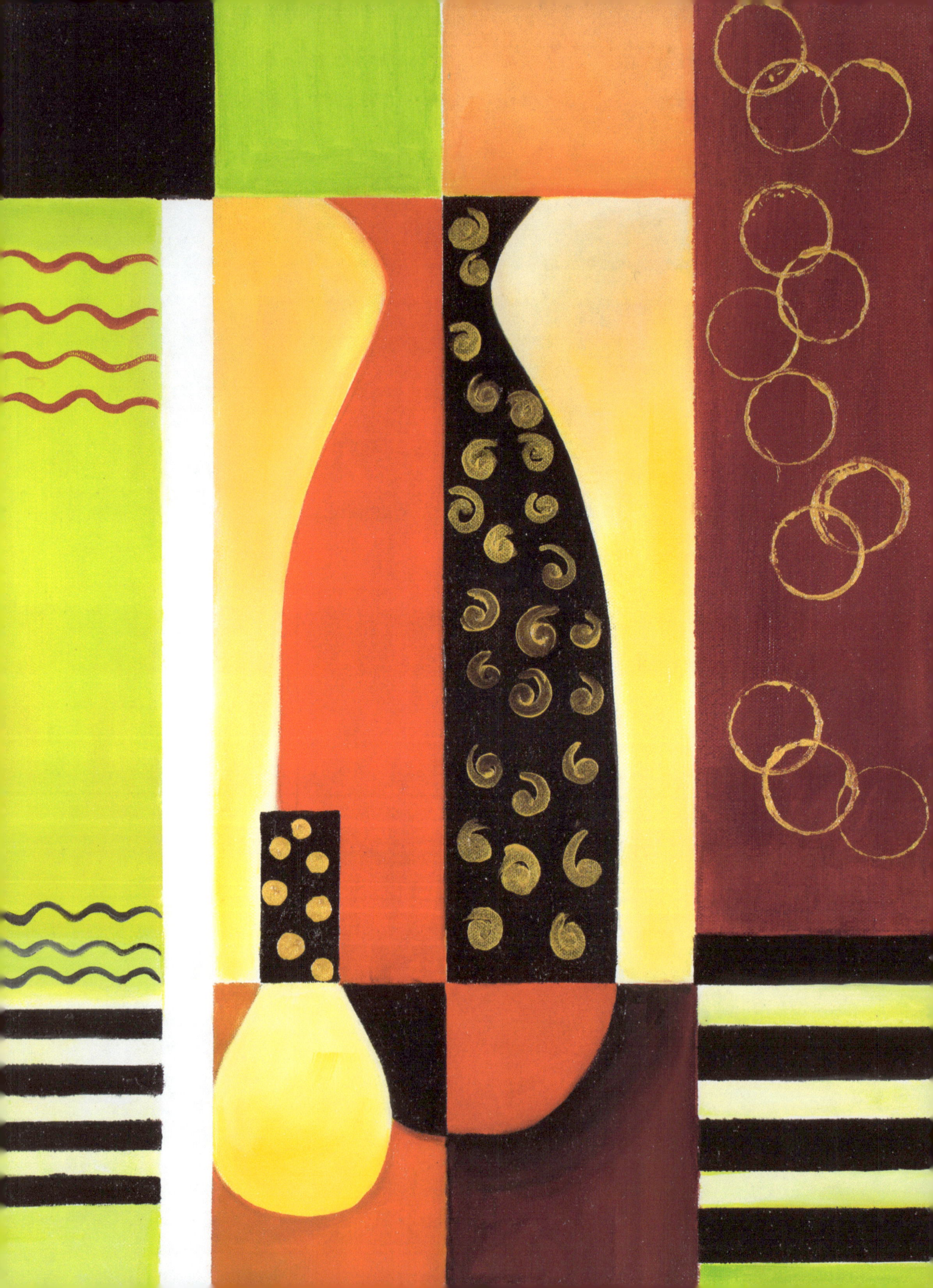

Geometrical Vases

A medley of colors
An array of shapes
Forming geometrical vases

Andrew Nazareth
Oil on canvas

Rocks in the Sea

Rocks teach us to stand tall
In times of joy and pain
Weathering stress and strain
No matter big or small

Michelle Nazareth
Acrylic finger-painting on glass

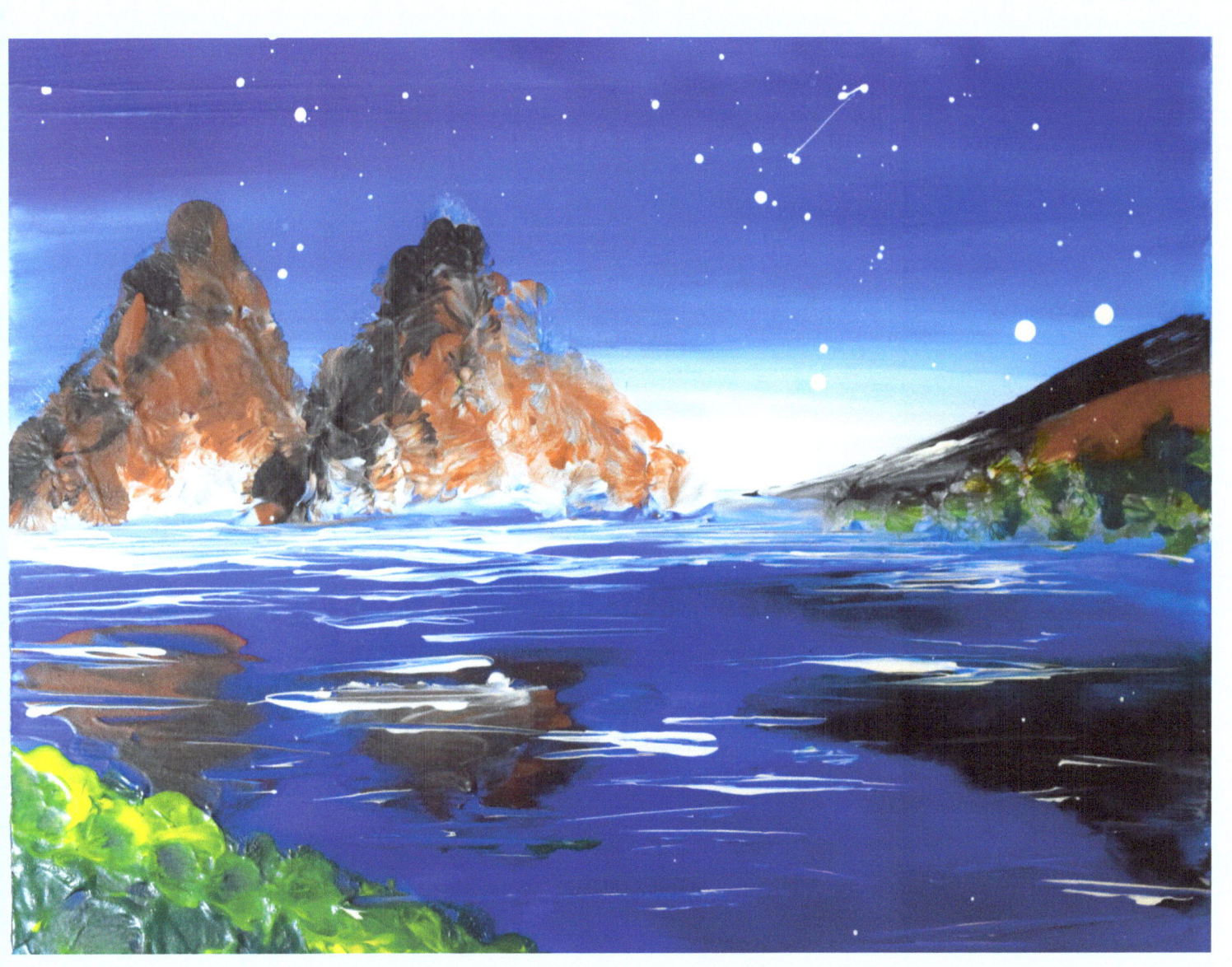

Sails

We adjust our life's sails
To flow with humanity
We love to blaze new trails
To show our deep sense of unity

Michelle Nazareth
Oil on canvas

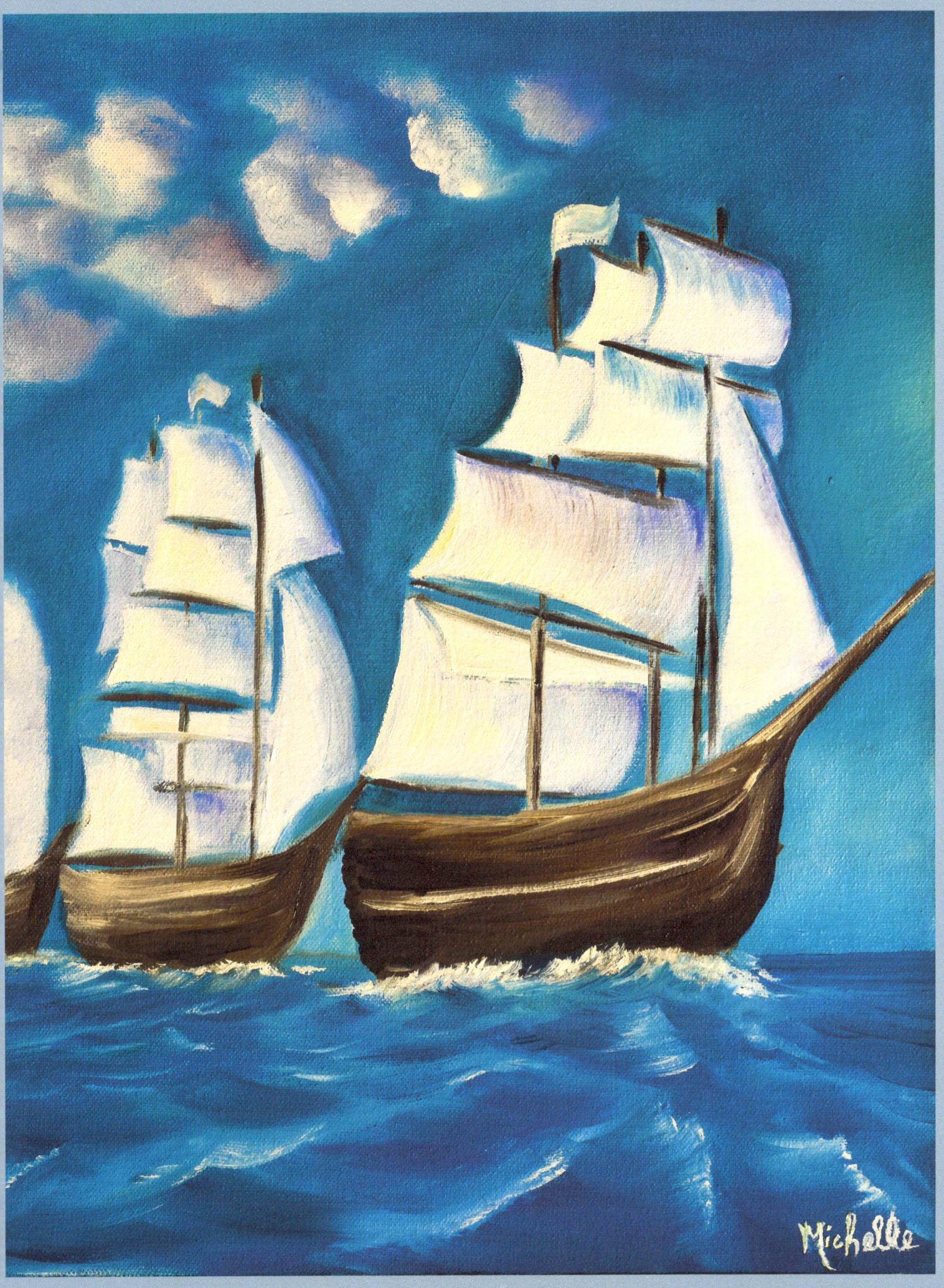

Trees by a Stream

Life flows gently
Like a stream
Gliding silently
In a quiet dream

Andrew Nazareth
Watercolor

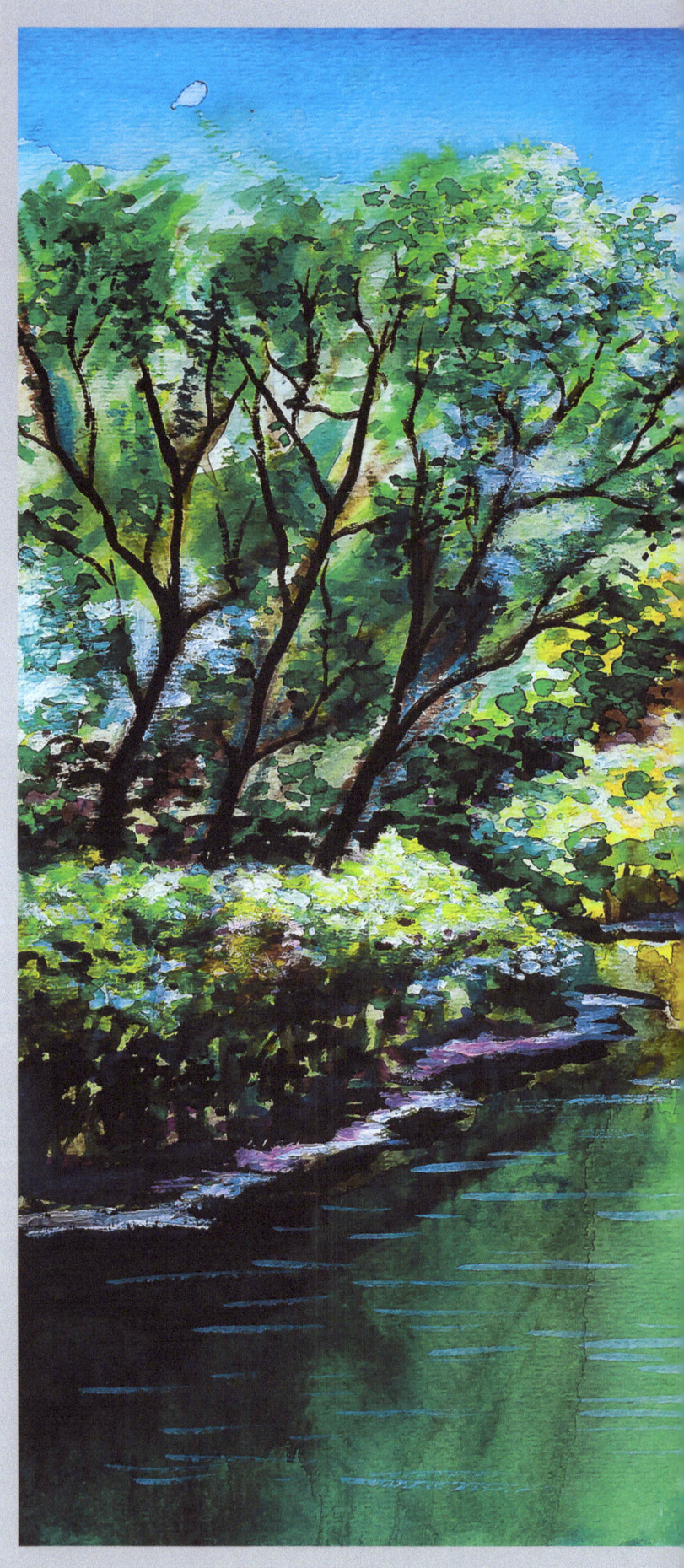

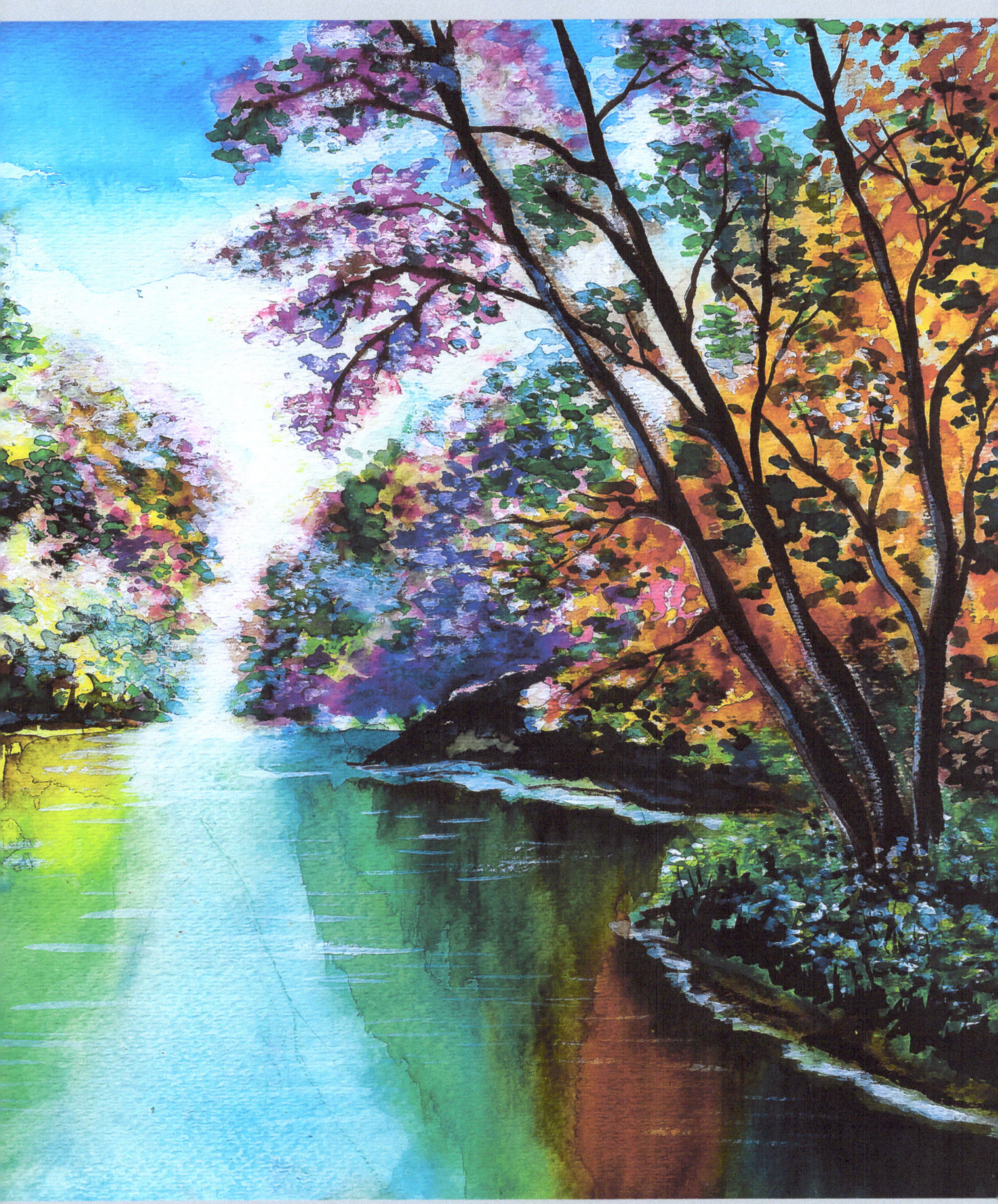

imagination

so daring
so deep
sometimes rigid
sometimes fluid...

Michelle Nazareth
Pour acrylic

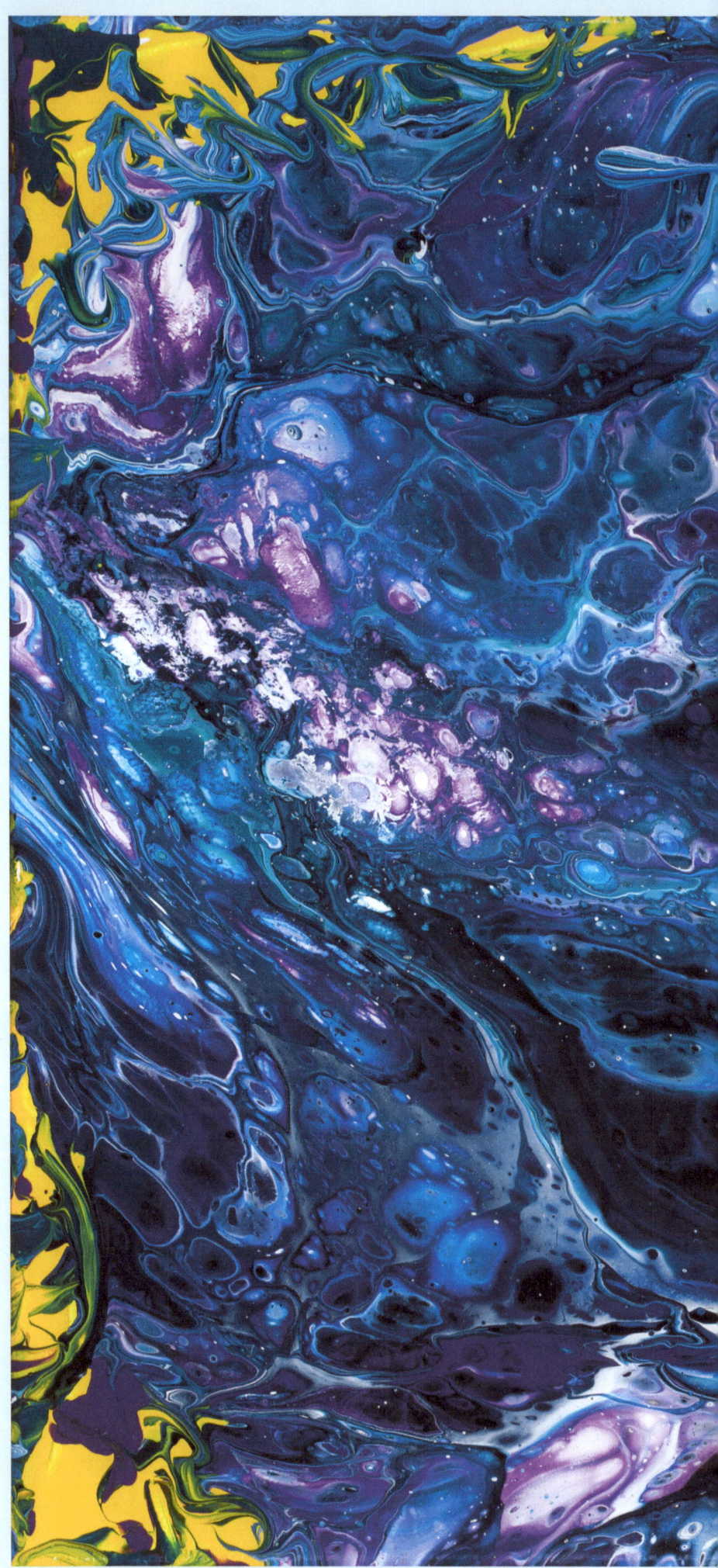

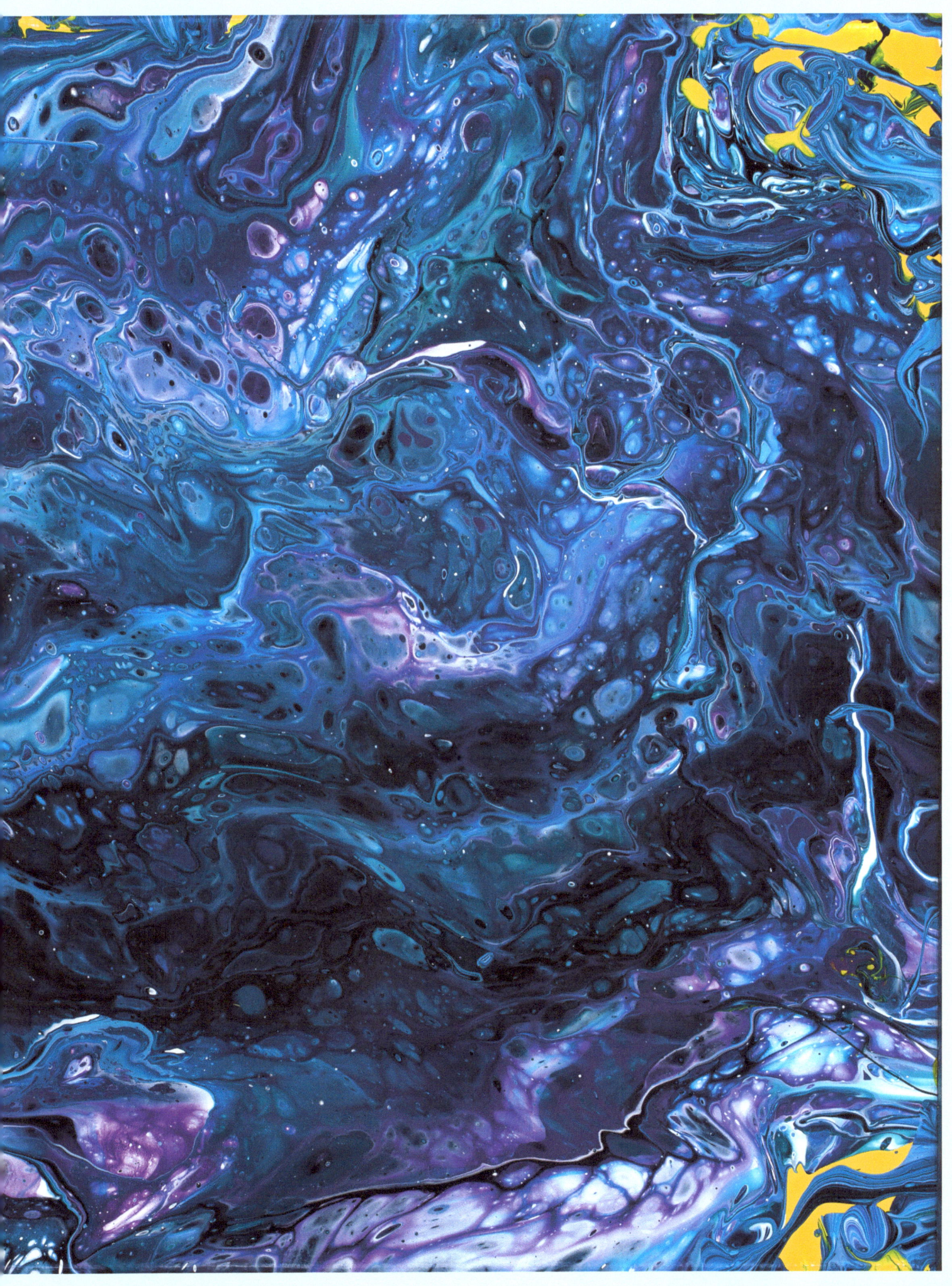

Fury

Nature's wrath and fury
Exposes human fragility
No progress o'er centuries
Can erase our dependability

Andrew Nazareth
Oil on canvas

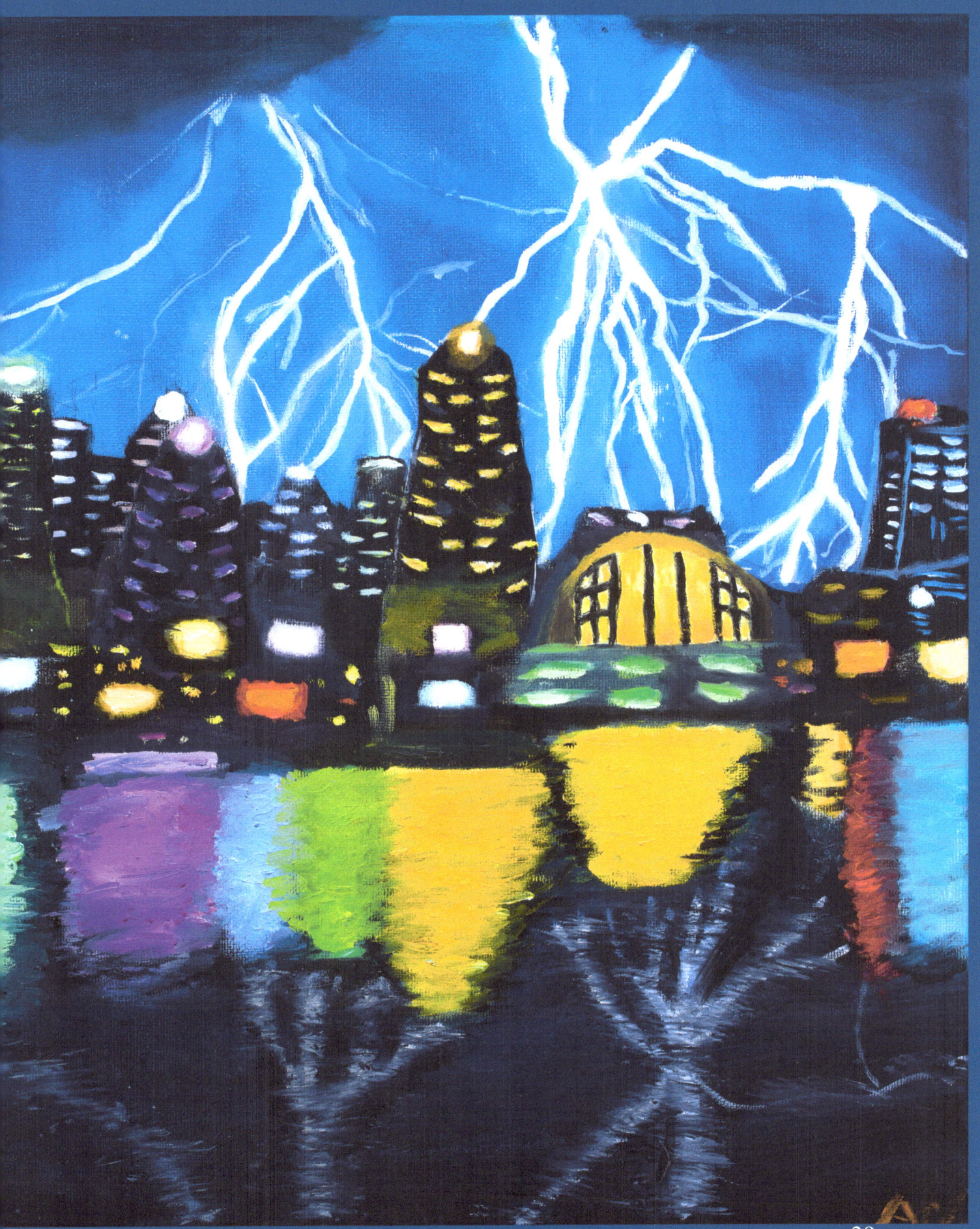

Flowers in a Vase

Flowers make you smile
Flowers mend broken hearts
Flowers remind us that
Life is worthwhile!

Michelle Nazareth
Oil on canvas

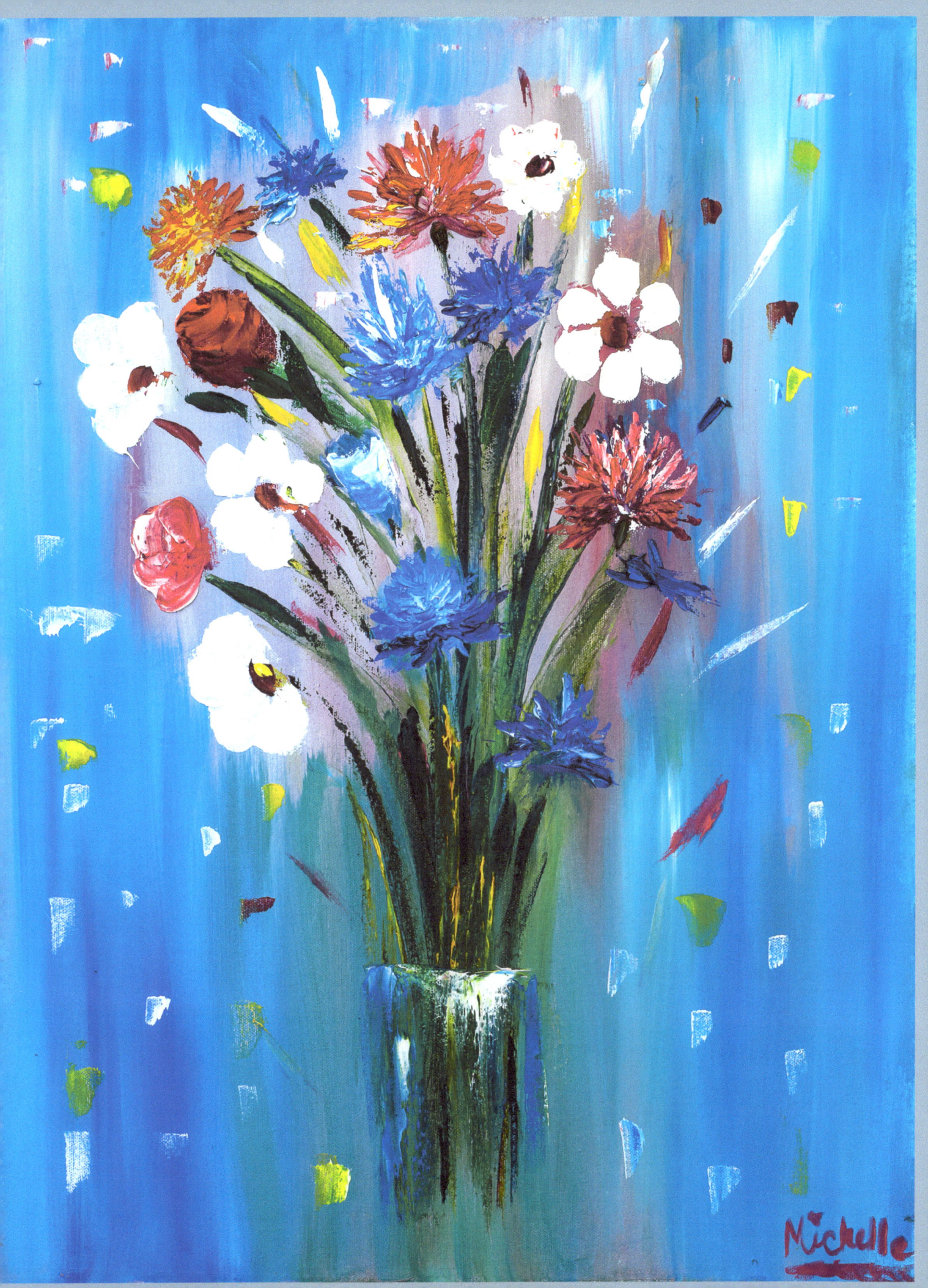

Italian Village

"Life is the secure ground of home, the sea is like life, the outside, the unknown."
—Stephen Gardiner

Andrew Nazareth
Watercolor

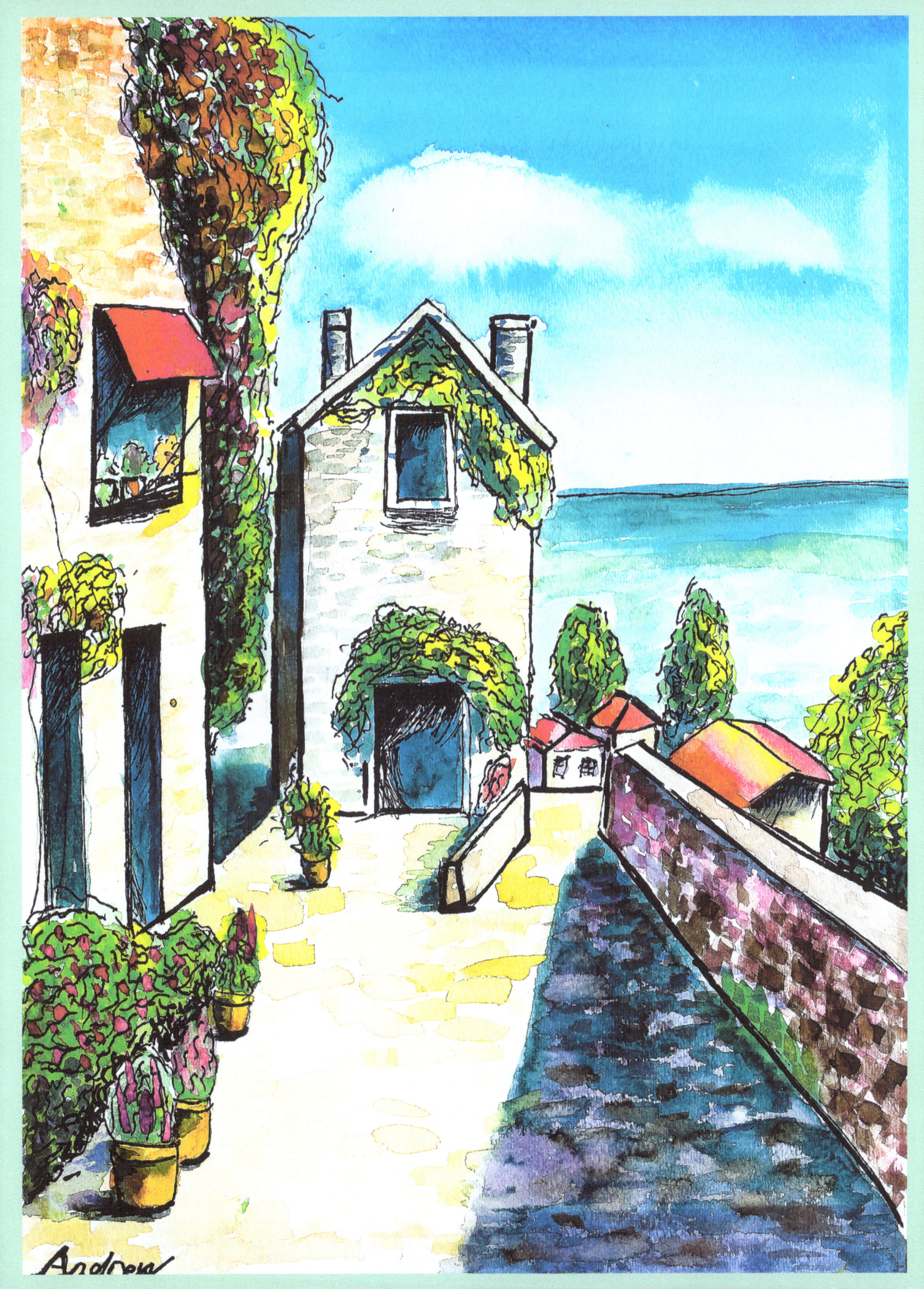

Strung on a String

On my windowsill
My balloon turns into the moon
Like a worm cocoons
To become a butterfly

Michelle Nazareth
Watercolor / Multimedia

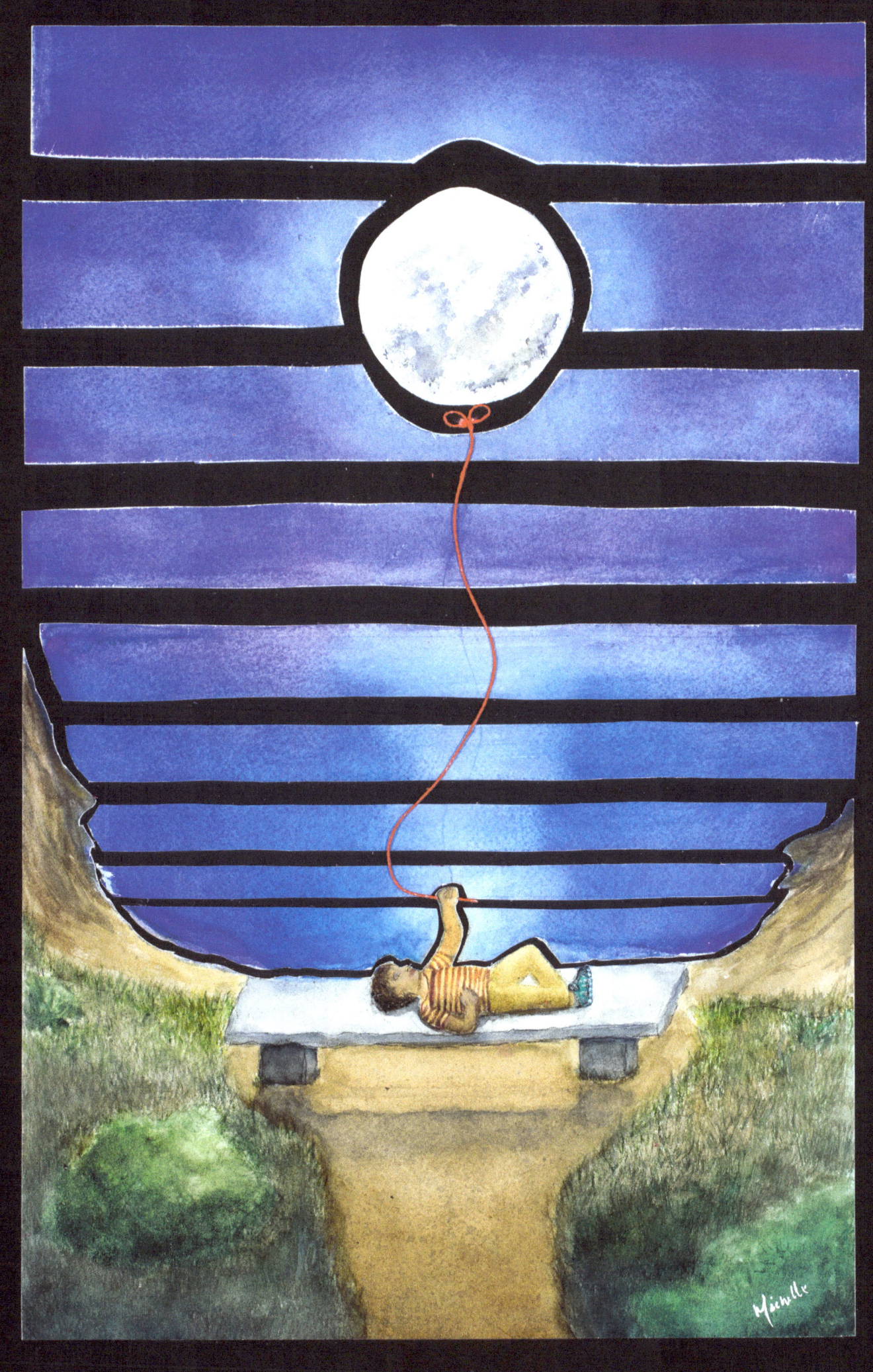

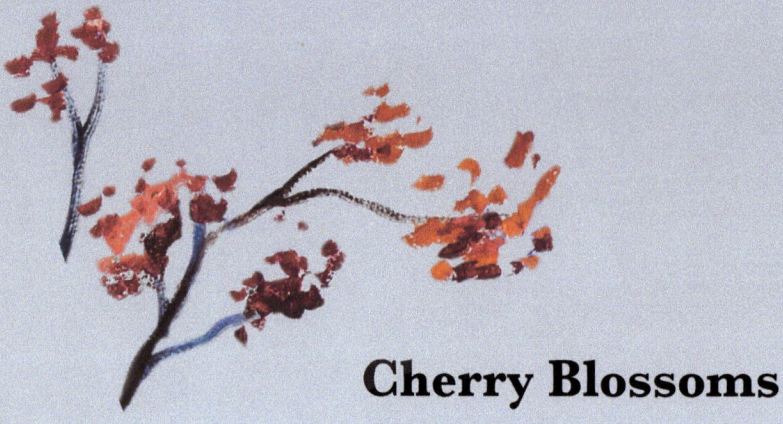

Cherry Blossoms

Cherry blossoms bloom
Soft and silky tenderness
Natural beauty

Andrew Nazareth
Oil on canvas

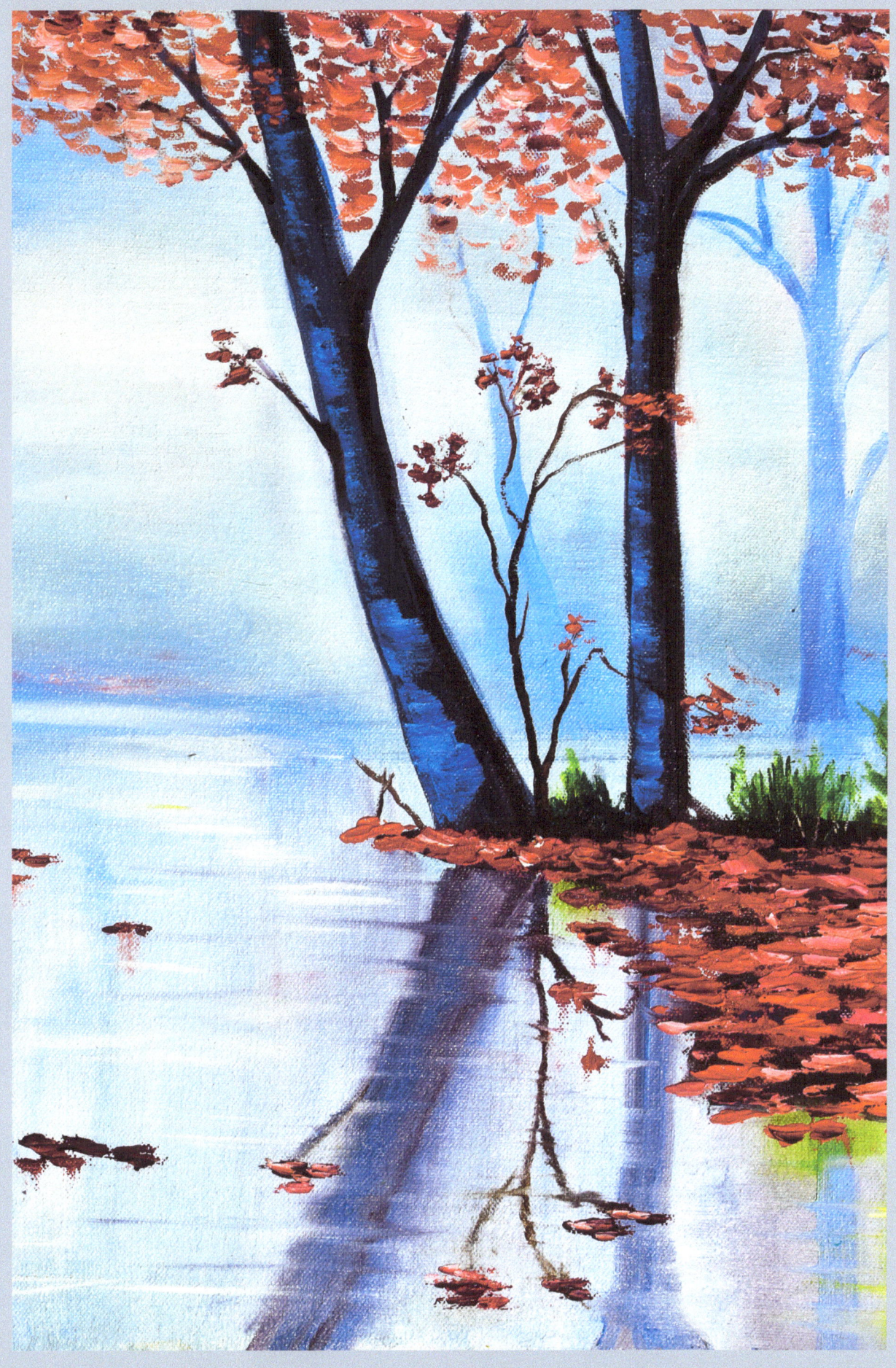

Bridge to Paradise

Calm, serene
Fleeting moments of happiness
Life is a canvas
Upon which we paint our bliss
Our bridge to paradise

Michelle Nazareth
Oil on canvas

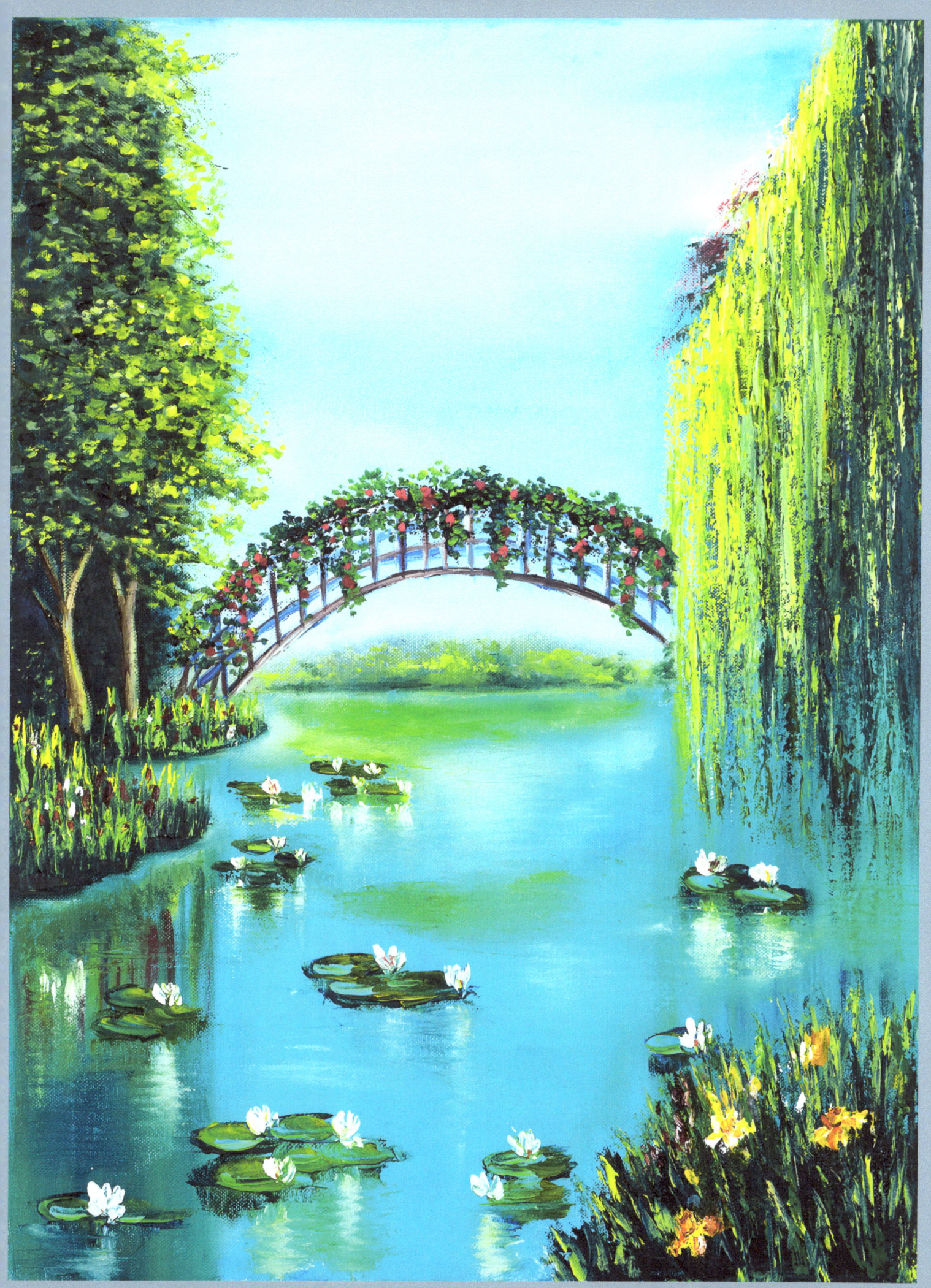

Flight of the Hummingbird

Be faithful in small things because it is in them that your strength lies
—Saint Teresa of Calcutta

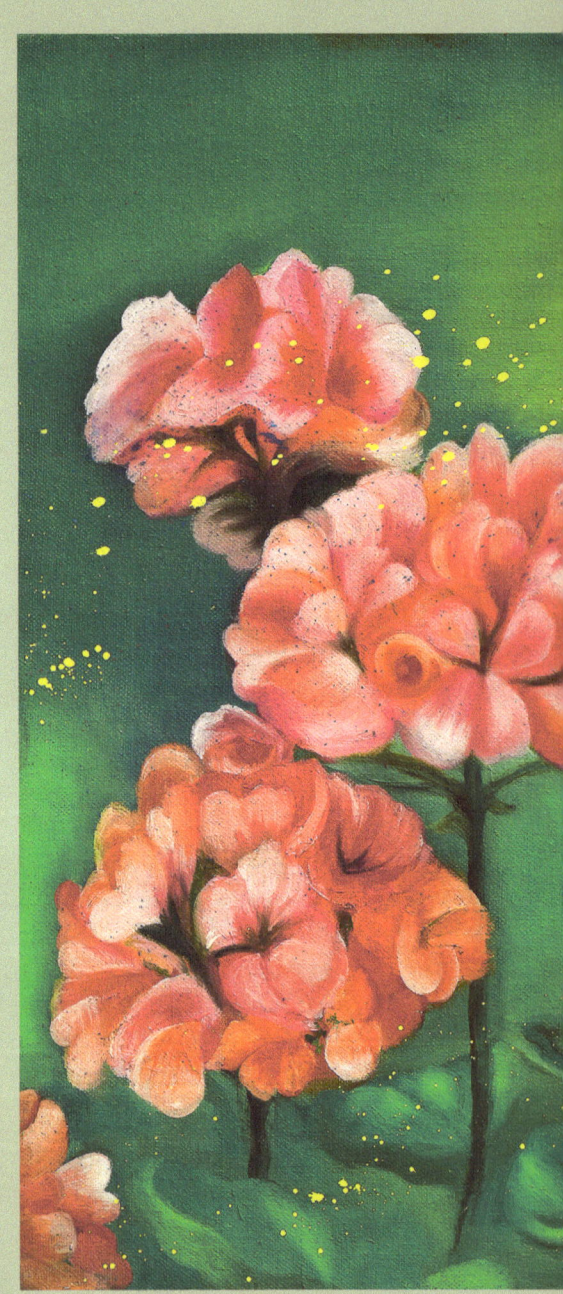

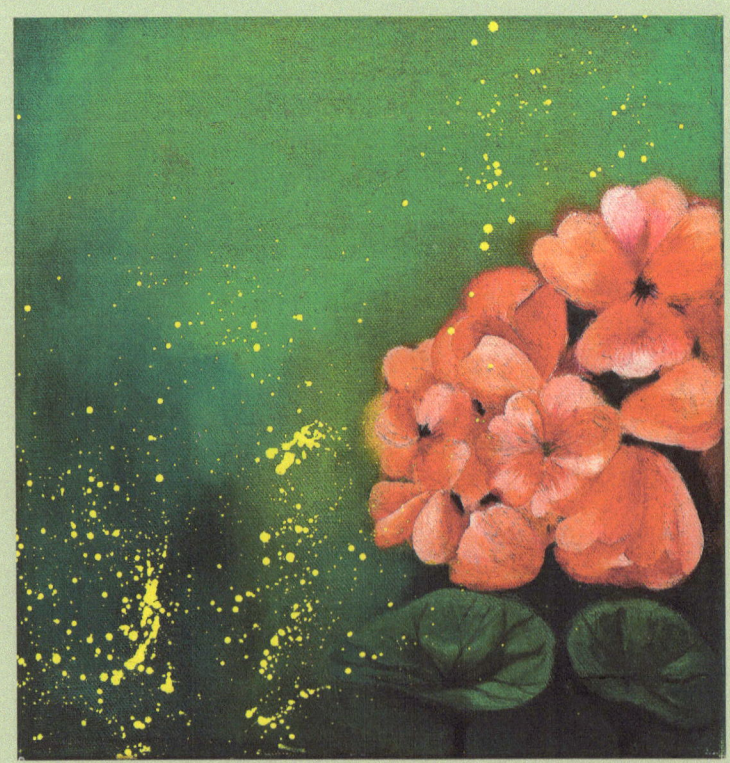

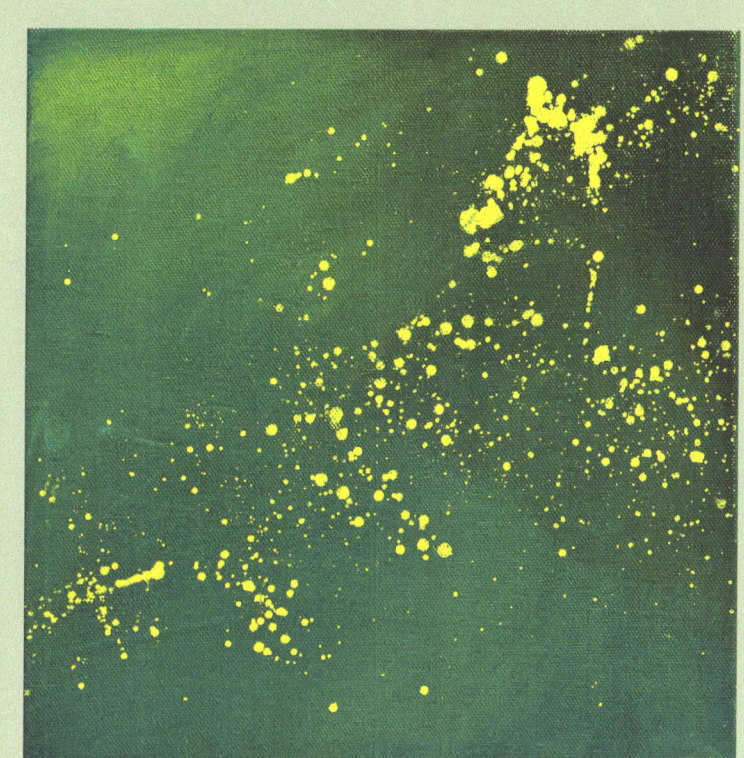
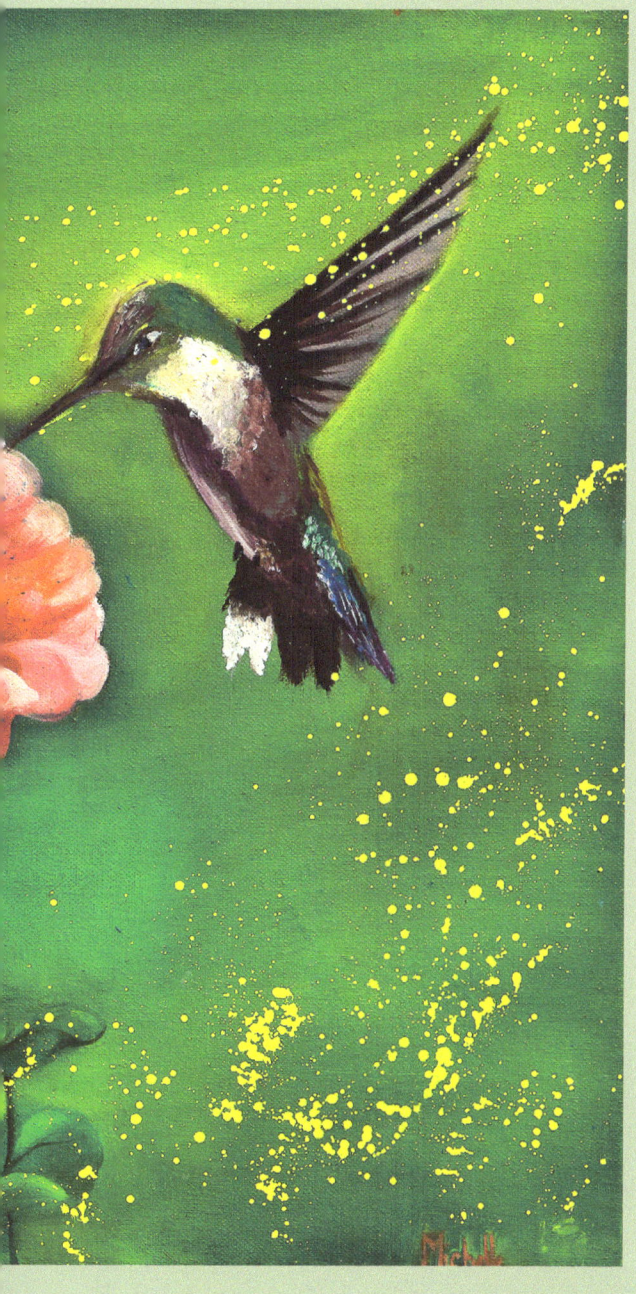

Michelle Nazareth
Oil on canvas

Northern Lights

Aurora Borealis
A symphony of colors
Swirls and dances
Over snowclad mountains
Serene
Magical
Reflecting God's glory

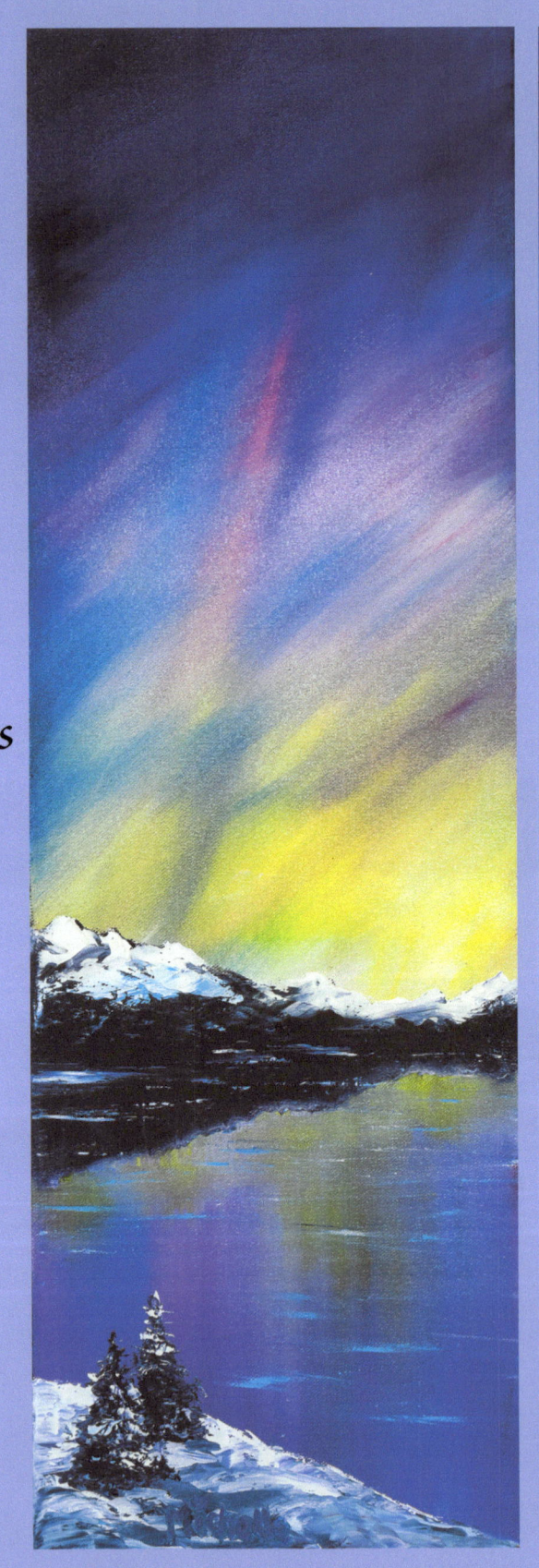

Northern Lights 1 (by Michelle)

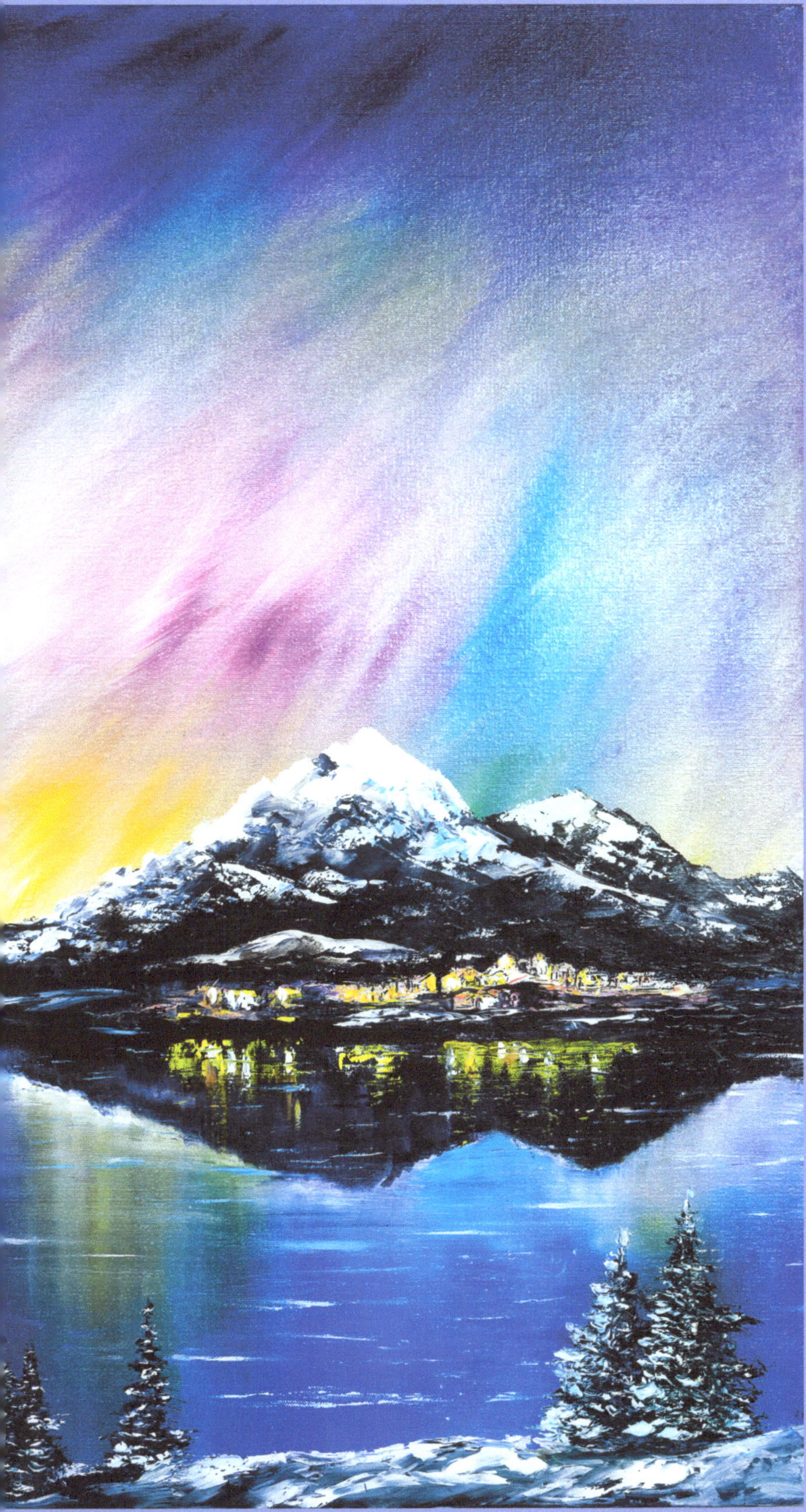

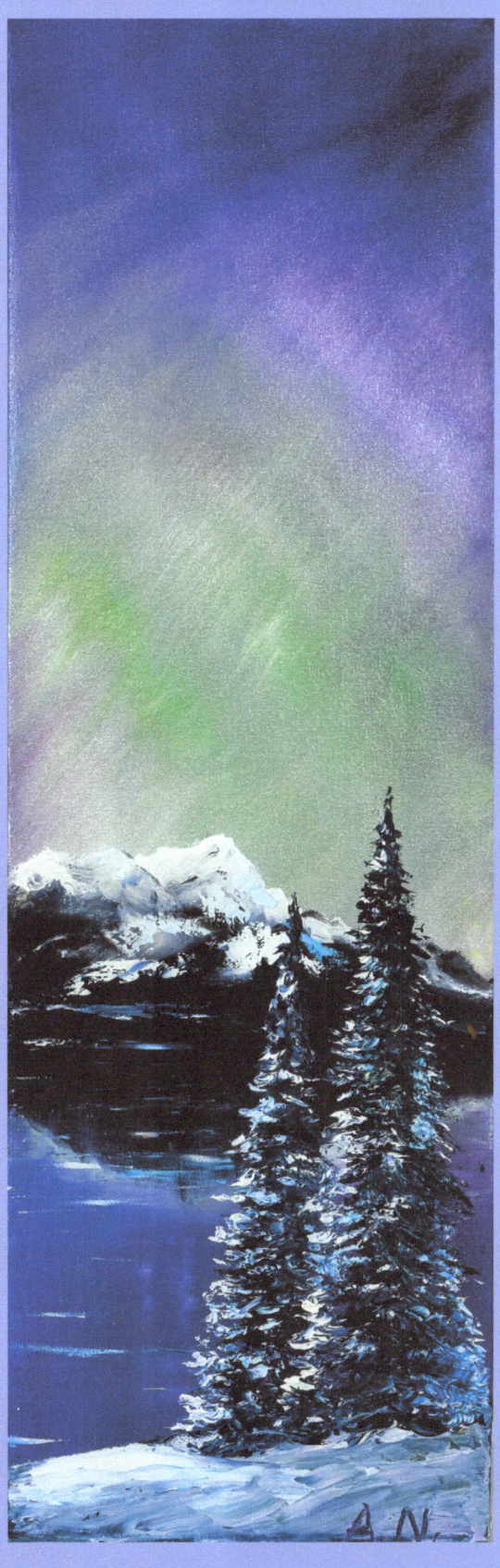

Northern Lights 2

(by Andrew and Michelle)

Northern Lights 3 (by Andrew)

About the Artists

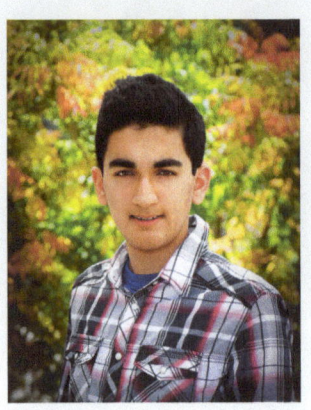 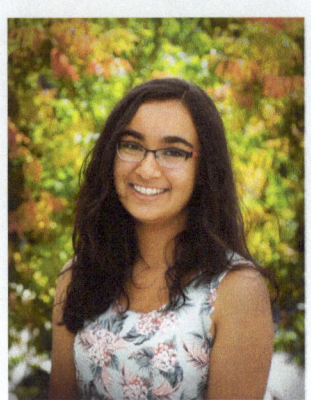

Andrew and Michelle Nazareth are national, state and county award winning teen artists and siblings who enjoy spreading hope through their art. They have been mentored for over a decade by their art teachers, Shirley Rhoades in Scotts Valley and Svetlana Semanova in San Jose, who have been instrumental in awakening their innate artistic talent. Andrew and Michelle prefer using oils, watercolors and pencil as media for their art. The themes of their paintings include seasonal landscapes, sci-fi, portraits and abstract material. Both Andrew and Michelle enjoy using realism as their artistic style. As anaphylactic allergy sufferers to peanut and other nuts, they feel fortunate for the treatment they received to desensitize them. As their way of paying it forward, Andrew and Michelle donate prints of their art to medical clinics, hold exhibitions in public spaces and use prints of their paintings for fund raisers and thank you cards, in their mission to allow their art to bring a smile to people's faces.

www.ingramcontent.com/pod-product-compliance
Lightning Source LLC
Chambersburg PA
CBHW051220220526
45473CB00003B/1109